The Trial of Pete

(Editor: Vincent Buranelli)

Alpha Editions

This edition published in 2024

ISBN : 9789362098269

Design and Setting By
Alpha Editions
www.alphaedis.com
Email - info@alphaedis.com

Preface

In this book you will find the reasons for the fame of Peter Zenger and Andrew Hamilton. You will also find the reason why James Alexander deserves mention as the third member of a great trio. Zenger was the central figure of a colorful and influential historical event—his trial for seditious libel. Hamilton was the champion who won him his freedom. The place of Alexander in all this is virtually unknown, and yet without him Hamilton's fame would be cut in half, while Zenger would not merit even a footnote in the histories of America, of democracy, or of journalism.

Alexander edited the *New York Weekly Journal*. That simple fact means that he was the first American editor to practice freedom of the press systematically and coherently, and the first to be justified legally. The defense of Zenger's person was a defense of Alexander's philosophy of journalism. The victory engineered by Hamilton was the result of a courtroom campaign along lines laid down by Alexander.

Perhaps it would be too strong to say that the genius behind the *Journal* was our greatest editor, but it would be hard to name one of equal importance. If we believe, as we do, that freedom of the press is essential to our civilization, surely we ought to give due recognition to the first American to say so and to act effectively. For this Scottish immigrant of the eighteenth century taught his adopted land the first law of sane journalism: that the news is to be reported on the basis of factual accuracy, and that censorship by the authorities is to be resisted as far as is consistent with national security and the interests of society.

The introduction to the text of the trial is based on a series of articles by the author, published in the following journals:

"Peter Zenger's Editor," *American Quarterly*, VII (1955), 174-81.

"Governor Cosby's Hatchet-Man," *New York History*, XXXVII (1956), 26-39.

"The Myth of Anna Zenger," *William and Mary Quarterly*, XIII (1956), 157-68.

"The Meaning of the Zenger Case," *Social Studies*, January, 1957.

"Governor Cosby and His Enemies," *New York History*, XXXVII (1956), 365-87.

"The Architect of Our Free Press," *Social Education*, XX (1956), 311-13.

For permission to use material from these articles, thanks are due to the respective editors and to the following societies: American Studies Association, New York State Historical Association, Institute of Early American History and Culture, and National Council for the Social Studies. The author also wishes to thank Mr. H. V. Kaltenborn, without whose Fellowship the research would never have been undertaken, much less published.

Foreword by H. V. Kaltenborn

My desk encyclopedia allots the subject of this book these two brief sentences: "Zenger, John Peter (1697-1749), American journalist, born Germany. His acquittal in libel trial helped further freedom of press in America."

That represents a very sober acknowledgment of the fact that the Zenger case established highly important precedents and is a landmark in the history of the free press among the English-speaking peoples of the world. With all this it is something of an anomaly that Peter Zenger never learned to write good English. He was not a newspaper editor, but only a printer who published the writings of others in an effort to earn an honest living. It was the incidental cause he served, rather than his professional work, that brought him his enduring fame.

He began his career as a printer's apprentice. He worked for William Bradford, the only printer in New York. Zenger became Bradford's partner, but soon established a business of his own, and since Bradford published the weekly newspaper that supported the British governor, it was only natural that those prominent members of the colony who opposed the governor should contract with Peter Zenger to print and publish a weekly paper for the opposition. Governor Cosby, whose word was law in the British colony of New York, was an arbitrary individual. As a personal representative of the British king he ran things pretty much as he pleased. His arbitrary acts helped create an opposition known as the Popular Party. Zenger's weekly became the organ for this party. Like other colonial newspapers of that day, it printed foreign news, literary essays, so called poetry, and a small amount of advertising. But its most interesting contents were the political articles attacking Governor Cosby and the actions of his administration. All these editorial comments were written by prominent members of the opposition party, but they were always signed with pen names.

Zenger's was the only name associated with the new opposition journal. Governor Cosby knew very well that Zenger was only the printer and had nothing to do with the paper's policy. He also knew that James Alexander, a brilliant leader of the political opposition, wrote or edited most of the articles that were critical of the Cosby administration. But the law, then as now, places responsibility on those who publish a libel—not upon those who write it. As a newspaper reporter, I myself once profited by that distinction. The *Brooklyn Daily Eagle* had to defend a one hundred thousand dollar libel suit for an article I had written. The leader of a religious sect that had its headquarters in Brooklyn was selling what it called Miracle Wheat. I exposed the one dollar a pound charge for this wheat as a fraud upon the public. That gave me the interesting task of helping the *Eagle's* lawyers prove with the help of agricultural experts the truth of my printed assertion. For today, as in the days since Peter Zenger's trial, the truth of the libelous allegations mitigates damages and justifies the libel.

It was not until the trial of Peter Zenger that his extremely able lawyer created the notable precedent that the truth must be accepted as justification for a libel and in mitigation of whatever damages might have been suffered by the plaintiff. In the *Brooklyn Eagle* Miracle Wheat case the libel was clear and the court so instructed the jury, which promptly brought in a verdict of six cents for the plaintiff. This justified the *Eagle* and humiliated the sellers of Miracle Wheat.

The Peter Zenger trial established one other notable precedent for libel cases. This was that the jury before which he was tried had the right not only to pass upon the fact but also the law in the case. The logic and eloquence of Zenger's attorney persuaded the jury that it had the right to determine how and to what extent the letter and spirit of the law could and should be applied in the Zenger case.

It is an interesting fact that the entire preceding history of the freedom of the press among English-speaking peoples played its part in the Zenger trial. The writings of Milton, Locke, Swift, Steele, Addison, and Defoe were all quoted to justify the freedom with which Zenger's newspaper voiced its criticism of Governor Cosby and the way he governed.

This willful executive first attempted to have Zenger indicted by a grand jury, but the jury refused to act. Then he ordered Zenger's paper to be burned by the public hangman, and it was duly burned, though not by the hangman. Finally the Governor secured the issue of a warrant for Zenger's arrest and the printer was put in jail on a charge of seditious libel. Zenger's journal missed a single issue. Then, thanks to his wife, it appeared every Monday while Zenger was in jail. Zenger's wife, Anna Catherine, took over the print shop and saw that the paper was published. She didn't write the contents any more than her husband, but she never complained that the printer's family was suffering for others.

Nowadays it is a Constitutional right that "Excessive bail shall not be required," but in Zenger's day there was no such rule. His bail was so high that neither he nor his friends could meet it. The fact that he was put in jail also helped sway public opinion in Zenger's favor.

The record of the Zenger trial as it is developed in this book is one of the notable case histories of American jurisprudence. Andrew Hamilton, Zenger's able attorney, made such a case for his client that it attracted attention not only in the colonies but in England. New York voted him the freedom of the city.

Governor Cosby did not long survive the rebuke he suffered by Zenger's acquittal. And here is a curious fact worth recalling: Andrew Hamilton, whose notable defense of Peter Zenger has become an imperishable part of the history of our free press, was also the architect of Independence Hall in Philadelphia. The Hall still stands and so does the decision in the Zenger case, both symbolizing enduring monuments to freedom.

Part One.
Introduction

1. The Causes of the Trial

I. Peter Zenger

Of all the personalities involved in the Zenger case, none eludes investigation so much as the man who gave his name to it. There are irritating lacunae in the biography of John Peter Zenger, and no artist ever found him worthy of sketch or portrait (at least none has survived), so that we do not even know his face. But this lack of information is by no means crippling to the historian of the period. If we would prefer to know more about Peter Zenger, the plain truth is that half a dozen other men were of more consequence than he in the establishment of a free press in New York. He was neither the editor of his newspaper nor even a principal writer for it during its great days; his function hardly went beyond that of the mere printer. He became famous almost by accident, famous as a symbol rather than as a motivating force. We can, therefore, "place" him with the less difficulty, and the data to hand are sufficient for that.

He was a German immigrant, a native of the Rhenish Palatinate, where he was born in 1697. His family brought him to the New World in 1710, and that same year he was apprenticed to William Bradford, the only printer then at work in New York, and one of the top men of his trade in the Colonies. Bradford's establishment was a good school for any apprentice, for it graduated a whole series of printers who became famous in their own right, the best remembered of whom was the master's son, Andrew Bradford, who competed with Benjamin Franklin for the publishing trade in Philadelphia.

Peter Zenger's indentures were for eight years, during which time he toiled at the Bradford press, beginning at the bottom as a typical ink-stained printer's devil and working his way up in the profession that Bradford liked to call "the art and mystery of printing." Peter never became a refined practitioner, for one reason because his grasp of the English language remained defective, but he came out of his training as skilled as many others in the field, and he was obeying a sound instinct when, his indentures up, he decided to strike out for himself as an independent.

During the years 1719-22 he wandered through the Colonies looking for a place to set up a permanent business. He married Mary White of Philadelphia, and had a son, John Zenger, who was a printer after him. His most ambitious venture took him to Maryland, where he became a citizen and was granted the right to publish the Colony's laws, proceedings, minutes, etc. What happened then is uncertain; perhaps it was just that his plans did not work out; perhaps the death of his wife was the crucial thing; for some reason he decided to abandon his Maryland career and return to New York. There he married his second wife, Anna Catherine Maulin, a native of Holland, and settled down for good.

In 1725 he joined William Bradford in a brief partnership, so brief that they published only one book jointly before splitting up, for what reason we do not know. The next year Peter Zenger went into business for himself, thus becoming the second printer in New York, and the first rival of his former master.

There was room for two. Bradford, the official printer, worked for the Governor, the Council, and the Assembly. He was an honest man, but understandably reluctant to jeopardize his position by turning out anything of which his patrons might disapprove. That was where Zenger came in. Proprietor of a second-class printing shop, cut off from government work, he could keep his head above water in only one way, by taking the trade of New Yorkers who had some motive for avoiding the official press, especially those who were dissatisfied with the situation in either Church or State and wanted to say so. For six years he supplemented his staple output (mainly religious tracts) with critical pamphlets and open letters. Gradually the logic of his predicament pushed him into the position of "official" printer to those writers whose material Bradford could not, or would not, touch.

Such was Zenger's status in the fall of 1732 when affairs in New York began to boil up into a political crisis that first involved him as a partisan in a duel of contending factions, and ultimately landed him in jail.

II. A Colonial Feud

The powder train for the explosion had been laid during the previous decade in the form of a savage feud between two of the most powerful families in New York—the Morrises and the Delanceys, led by the patriarchs Lewis Morris and Stephen Delancey. Fundamentally, the conflict was the primordial one between landed gentry and business tycoons, and the occasion produced two perfect representatives to act as leaders.

Lewis Morris—territorial aristocrat, councillor, assemblyman, chief justice of the Supreme Court—was the model of the wealthy, influential, proud, and ambitious colonial magnate. He made his family great, and handed on the tradition to his more famous grandsons, Gouverneur Morris and the Lewis Morris who signed the Declaration of Independence. He was a commanding figure in the politics of both New York and New Jersey, headstrong in defense of himself, his family, and his class, and a power for any governor to reckon with.

Stephen Delancey stood for the ever-increasing authority of money. He was New York's leading merchant prince, a self-made man who accumulated a fortune in trade with Canada. French by birth, he was a Huguenot by religion, with all the tenacious acquisitiveness and flinty Puritan morality of his sect. In the Assembly he spoke for the powerful mercantile clique, and that alone would have made him—hardly less than Lewis Morris—a dangerous man to cross.

Now Morris crossed Delancey, and did it in two peculiarly galling ways. First of all, from the floor of the Assembly he led an attack on the trade in which the entrepreneur had made his money. Under this commercial system, New York businessmen sent their wares directly to the French in Canada, who used the manufactured articles they received to carry on their fur trade with the Indians. The system was a very profitable one for many New Yorkers, but Governor William Burnet was anxious to end it because it strengthened the hand of the French with the Indians, making the latter reliant on Quebec instead of Albany. Morris acted as his manager in the Assembly during the furious controversy that followed, while Stephen Delancey naturally commanded the opposition. The struggle developed into a fierce personal rivalry that continued to move with its own momentum long after Delancey had triumphed over Morris in this case of the Canada trade.

Secondly, Morris seems to have instigated Governor Burnet to question Delancey's right to sit in the Assembly on the ground that he was a foreigner, a purely personal attack of so little validity that the Governor had to back down and apologize to the Chamber for usurping one of its prerogatives, after which it put its seal of approval on Stephen Delancey.

There is no need to explain at length how the old plutocrat reacted to these insults. We simply note that the perspicacious

Cadwallader Colden terms Delancey "a man of strong and lasting resentments" and adds that the Morris-Delancey clash gave rise to "violent party struggles." Before long New York was disturbed by hostile groups known from their chiefs as the "Morris Interest" and the "Delancey Interest." This is the background to the Zenger case. Party alignment was obviously dictated in many cases by motives other than personal allegiance—by political, social, and economic factors—but for our purposes the fundamental thing is the Morris-Delancey antithesis. During Burnet's administration (1720-28) these embittered Interests were engaged in a constant struggle for power, with the Morrisites strong because they had the ear of the Governor, and the Delanceyites because the Assembly swung over to their side.

With the regime of Governor John Montgomerie (1728-31), the Delancey Interest definitely became paramount in New York because this executive made it the cornerstone of his policy to stay on good terms with the Assembly. Montgomerie maintained an uneasy peace (partly because he was himself a rather feckless individual), but the atmosphere in New York did not thereby cease to be explosive, for the Morris Interest, although temporarily checked, was still powerful, still ambitious, still hopeful, and still watching for the pendulum to swing its way.

Thus the scene was set for a violent climax whenever a sufficient cause should appear. It appeared on Montgomerie's death in the person of the new governor, Colonel William Cosby.

III. Governor Cosby

If you look into Burke's *Landed Gentry of Great Britain and Ireland*, you will find the following paragraph embedded in the genealogical history of "Cosby of Stradbally":

William, brigadier-general, col. of the royal Irish, governor of New York and the Jersies, equerry to the Queen, and m. Grace, sister of George Montague Earl of Halifax, K.B., and left by that lady (who d. 25 Dec. 1767) at his decease, 10 March 1736, the following issue, William, an officer in the Army; Henry, R.N., d. 1753; Elizabeth, m. to Lord Augustus Fitzroy, 2nd son of Charles, Duke of Grafton; Anne, m. to —— Murray, Esq. of New York.

The entry enables us to form a pretty good idea of the background from which Governor Cosby came and explains much of his behavior as chief executive of New York. He was an Anglo-Irish aristocrat, sprung from the notorious Ascendancy class that maintained its position through a whole series of penal laws designed to keep the majority of Irishmen in subjection. He had all the craving for place and pension, the haughtiness, and the venal devotion to the *status quo* that were common in the worst section of his class, and these vices merely perverted a strong will and a certain resourcefulness in meeting obstacles.

With intelligence and decency William Cosby might have been a man of fair ability; instead he became a sycophant with his superiors, an intriguer with his equals, and a petty tyrant with those beneath him. We know from his correspondence that he could not abide opposition or even criticism.

How much of a soldier he was remains doubtful since, although he rose to the rank of general, it was a period in which office frequently enough went with bribery, conniving, and influence rather than with ability. William Cosby was in a position to resort to all of these because he enjoyed powerful contacts in England, being a close friend of the Duke of Newcastle, while his wife was a sister of the Earl of Halifax. These noblemen may both have been instrumental in furthering his rise in the army. His administrative career in the Colonies was certainly largely due to Newcastle, who controlled the Board of Trade and was able to send out whom he chose.

Cosby's first governorship took him to the island of Minorca, where his high-handedness and cupidity exasperated the Minorcans, and they protested repeatedly to the Board of Trade. He committed one crime that London could not overlook or minimize: while England and Spain were at peace in 1718 Cosby ruthlessly seized the goods of a Spanish merchant, ordered them sold at auction, and then manipulated the records to cover his tracks. The whole thing was too flagrant. The Governor was ordered to reimburse his victim and removed from his post in Minorca.

Notwithstanding the incident, Cosby was able to wangle other appointments, of which the New York governorship was the most important. The feeling of the Colonials when they learned of the Minorca affair was expressed by Cadwallader Colden:

How such a man, after such a flagrant instance of tyranny and robbery, came to be intrusted with the government of an English colony and to be made Chancellor and keeper of the King's conscience in that colony, is not easy for a common understanding to conceive without entertaining thoughts much to the disadvantage of the honor and integrity of the King's Ministers, otherwise than by thinking that the Ministry believed that what he had suffered by the complaints made against him from Minorca would make him for the future carefully avoid giving any occasion of complaint from his new government.[1]

However, there was no local prejudice against the new Governor when he arrived on August 1, 1732. His Minorca past was unknown. He had had the shrewdness to ingratiate himself with New Yorkers, while he lingered in England for over a year, by agitating against the pending sugar bill as detrimental to Colonial commercial interests; he was unable to bring news of success with him, but at least he was believed to have tried, and this alone would have created an atmosphere favorable to him. He had, moreover, personal attributes calculated to make him popular in Colonial society—a smooth charm, good birth, high military rank, familiar connections with the nobility at home, and a wife who was the sister of an earl. He was fond of playing the host on a lavish scale, and the parties and dances at the Governor's mansion were soon noted as among the gayest ever seen in New York City.

IV. The Governor and His Enemies

Given all this popularity and good will on his arrival, what was it that went wrong? How did William Cosby's become "one of the most disturbed administrations in New York Colonial history"? The transition was very rapid. Within three months of his arrival the new Governor wrote to the Duke of Newcastle:

I am sorry to inform your Grace that the example and spirit of the Boston people begin to spread amongst these colonies in a most prodigious manner. I had more trouble to manage these people than I could have imagined; however for this time I have done pretty well with them; I wish I may come off as well with them of the Jersies.[2]

That old bugbear of Colonial governors, trouble with the Assembly, was not in question. Unlike many men better than himself, Cosby got along very well with his legislature, his differences with it being hardly more than the inevitable friction created by two forces in contact and working toward ends that did not always coincide. The harmony was striking because he insulted the Assembly after it had voted him a present for his opposition to the sugar bill: the sum did not satisfy him, and he snarled to Lewis Morris, "Damn them, why did they not add shillings and pence? Do they think that I came from England for money? I'll make them know better."[3]

- 14 -

This was a gratuitous affront, and typical of the small-minded avaricious man who offered it, but it did not raise any political issue that could cause a quarrel.

The quarrel began within the Governor's Council, among the men who were supposed to be his close intimate advisers. The predisposing condition already existed there in the form of the Morris-Delancey feud, on the smoldering embers of which Cosby proceeded to pour oil. From the Council, ripples of animosity spread through the Colony, dividing the people into two factions—the Court party of the Governor (which absorbed the Delancey Interest), and the Popular party (formerly the Morris Interest) of his enemies. It happened like this.

During the year that Cosby stayed on in England after his appointment, the leadership of New York devolved on the president of the Council, the ranking member, who happened to be a veteran of the old New Amsterdam days named Rip Van Dam. He was a hard-headed, tight-fisted, honest Dutchman, not very able, but extremely devoted to his duties and his rights. During his tenure of office he was voted, and drew, the stipend attached to it.

When Cosby finally arrived on the scene, he produced a royal decree ordering Van Dam to divide the sum with him. Van Dam's answer was a shrewd reprisal. Knowing that Cosby had received many emoluments of the governorship while in England, he suggested a division that would include these, and he calculated that on this basis the Governor actually owed him a substantial amount. The dictatorial proconsul rejected the proposal with all the anger and contempt he usually displayed when thwarted. He decided to sue.

Determined to keep the case away from a jury because of local sentiment that favored a Colonial against a crown official, and unable to proceed in chancery since he would be presiding as chancellor over his own suit, Cosby hit on the idea of letting the justices of the Supreme Court handle it as Barons of the Exchequer. He therefore named the Supreme Court a court of equity, after which he brought suit against Van Dam.

The defendant's lawyers were James Alexander and William Smith, two of the foremost members of the New York bar, who had been advising him throughout. When the suit began in the new court of equity, Alexander and Smith adopted the bold course of denying the validity of the court itself, arguing in particular that it was illegal for the Governor to establish it of his own free will and without the consent of the Assembly. This plea was more than an attack on the jurisdiction of a court: it was a direct accusation that the Governor had overstepped the limits of his authority and had violated the law.

The three justices of the Supreme Court were divided on the merits of the plea. Two of them, James Delancey and Frederick Philipse, rejected it out of hand. They belonged to the Governor's faction. But the Chief Justice was of another mind, and that was the critical thing, for he was Lewis Morris. (Notice the names. We are back in the familiar atmosphere of the Morris-Delancey feud, James being the son of old Stephen Delancey.) Morris had opposed obnoxious governors in the past, and he would not back down before Governor Cosby. There was this added point about Lewis Morris, that he had functioned in the New Jersey Council as did Van Dam in New York's, so his pocketbook stood in the same kind of jeopardy if Van Dam should be condemned.

The Chief Justice therefore agreed with the counsel for the defense that the court of equity was no true court, and he openly defied the Governor with these words:

I take it the giving of a new jurisdiction in Equity by letters patent to an old Court that never had such jurisdiction before, or erecting a new Court of Equity by letters patent or ordinances of the Governor and Council, without assent of the legislature, are equally unlawful, and not a sufficient warrant to justify this Court to proceed in a course of Equity. And therefore by the grace of God, I, as Chief Justice of this Province, shall not pay any obedience to them in that point.[4]

The Governor was away in New Jersey at the time but, hearing what had happened, he wrote Morris a furious and insulting letter, and demanded a copy of the remarks he had made in court. The Chief Justice complied, at the same time publishing the remarks (through the Zenger press) as a gesture of studied contempt for all the Colony to see. This was more than Cosby was willing to stand. On May 3, 1733, he wrote to the Duke of Newcastle:

Things are now gone that length that I must either discipline Morris or suffer myself to be affronted, or, what is still worse, see the King's authority trampled on and disrespect and irreverence to it taught from the Bench to the people by him who, by his oath and his office, is obliged to support it. This is neither consistent with my duty nor my inclination to bear, and therefore when I return to New York I shall displace him and make Judge Delancey Chief Justice in his room.[5]

In August, Cosby made good his threat. At one Council meeting, and without notifying Morris in advance, he announced that henceforth Delancey was chief justice of the Supreme Court of New York, with Philipse advancing to the second place. Cadwallader Colden, who was present in his capacity of councillor, tells us that he disapproved of the Governor's action, and that Cosby resented his saying so. Colden's account of the episode is so revealing of Cosby's character that it is worth quoting in full:

I had been sent for to town a few days before under pretense of some affairs in my office of Surveyor General. When I came into the Governor's house he received me into his arms with, "My dear Colden, I am glad to see you." I was caressed for two or three days by every one of the family. Just before I went to Council he took me upon the couch and seemed to entertain me in the most friendly manner, but spoke not one word of removing the Chief Justice and appointing another till we were sitting in Council, when he said that he had removed Mr Morris and appointed James Delancey in his room, and thought this the most proper place to give the first notice of it. Upon which I said, "Then Your Excellency only tells us what you have already done?" To which he answered, "Yes." I replied, "It is not what I would have advised." And he very briskly returned to it, "I do not ask your advice." This put his having the consent of the Council out of the question and defeated the whole design he had been put upon of cajoling me (for I do not think he was capable of forming any design himself that had any reach). However he never forgave me.[6]

Morris soon learned what had taken place at the meeting, and in a letter of protest he passed the information on to London:

I believe I am well informed that, on the delivery of the Commissions to the Judges in Council, Doctor Colden asked the Governor whether the Council was summoned to be advised on that head? If they were, he would advise against it as being prejudicial to His Majesty's service. To which the Governor replied that he did not, nor ever intended to, consult them about it; he thought fit to do it, and was not accountable to them; or words to that effect.[7]

From this time on there was no mollifying Lewis Morris. Implacably revengeful, he never lowered his sights from two main goals, to regain the office of chief justice, and to get William Cosby removed from the governorship of New York. He achieved neither of these, but he did achieve the leadership of the antiadministration faction—the Popular party—that gave Cosby no peace.

The Governor had really stirred up a hornets' nest. Not only was New York already disgusted with him as a man and an executive, his private arrogance and public avarice being notorious, but he had openly adopted the pattern of behavior that had made Colonial governors unpopular in the past. Before he finished he had insulted the Assembly, tampered with the courts, divided his Council into venomous cliques, frightened property owners with his claims to land, and treated leading citizens with cavalier disdain. He practiced nepotism, tried to rig elections, and violated his instructions from London.

He committed a blunder as well as a crime when he alienated some of the most powerful men in his Colony—especially Lewis Morris, Rip Van Dam, and James Alexander, the last of whom became the mastermind of the Popular party. Working with them were Colden, William Smith, Lewis Morris, Junior, and many others down the scale into the anonymous mass of the population. The opposition to Governor Cosby soon turned from a matter of sporadic pinpricks into a concerted conspiracy bent on his political destruction.

The Governor's friends rallied around him, led by Chief Justice James Delancey (the only man of real ability among them), but they suffered in the contest for public opinion because they had to defend Cosby at a time when New Yorkers generally had made up their minds that he was indefensible. However, the Court party was strong in this, that it possessed the governmental machinery that could be brought to bear at a dozen different points of the battlefield, for example in the magistracies and at the bar.

V. The Administration Newspaper

The Court party also possessed the only newspaper in the Colony, William Bradford's *New York Gazette*. Bradford himself was hardly a party man, but (again as official printer) he was in no position to let his little two-page publication be used against those in power. He could not refuse to let them censor the *Gazette*. He could not even demur when Governor Cosby decided to put one of his own men in charge of editorial policy.

That decision introduces us to the most entertaining rascal of the Zenger case—Francis Harison, the dubious individual who functioned as editor-by-appointment and flatterer-in-chief to His Excellency the Governor. Since Harison was a censor in fact, if not in name, he merits some attention in any explanation of how freedom of the press was established for the first time on this side of the Atlantic. His career, more than any except Governor Cosby's, reveals why the Popular party of New York determined to throw down the gauntlet in the form of an opposition newspaper.

Francis Harison was notorious before Cosby was ever heard of in the Colony. Arriving more than twenty years earlier, he soon carved out a comfortable niche for himself. He had an enormous gift for wheedling jobs of some importance, and he did very well for himself, becoming among other things a member of the Governor's Council, recorder for the City of New York, and a judge of the admiralty. He served as one of the commissioners in settling the boundary dispute with Connecticut. He must have been a real genius at wangling, for on more than one occasion he showed a dishonesty and a stupidity so startling as to rouse wonder that anyone ever trusted him with responsibility.

Take the matter of the Connecticut boundary, when he stumbled on the chance for his first really outrageous performance, an act as characteristic of the man as anything you could ask for. Knowing that 50,000 acres were to be turned over to New York in one place (the famous "Oblong"), he wrote clandestinely to friends in London, urging them to snap up the land before local people could get their hands on it. At the same time he maneuvered himself into the group of Colonials who were applying for a patent, apparently with the intention of undermining his trusting and unsuspecting colleagues, and of wresting control from them as agent for the London syndicate.

If such duplicity was second nature to him, its outcome was no less typical. The London patentees, after hurriedly obtaining a royal grant according to the advice of their mentor in New York, discovered that he (a boundary commissioner, be it remembered) had given them misplaced lines on the map, and that their claim was already occupied. How they felt about him after that may easily be surmised, also how the New Yorkers reacted to his perfidy. From then on it was axiomatic that when dealing with Francis Harison you had to use extreme caution and circumspection.

If we judge by intent and motive rather than by accomplishment, he was as consummate a scoundrel as the Colonies ever produced. His only saving grace was a beguiling habit of being almost invariably hoist with his own petard. Stupid criminality followed by exposure and humiliation—that is the pattern; and wherever you find it on the banks of the Hudson during the early 1730's, you may justifiably look for the imprint of Francis Harison's fine Italian hand.

His big opportunity came with the arrival of Colonel Cosby. The two hit it off from the start. They were two of a kind, complementaries: the one found a willing tool, the other a powerful patron. Where the Governor was perforce hemmed in to a certain extent by the nature of his office, his lieutenant enjoyed a wide latitude where he could do almost as he pleased.

In the Cosby scheme of things Harison was allotted the dirty work, the low chicanery, and the brute force that the administration resorted to. In particular, he was given control of the *Gazette*, to which he fed weekly eulogies of the administration. His associates may have despised him privately (we know that James Delancey did), but in the governor's mansion he received the appreciation due his special talents. Cosby, like many another tyrant, had a place near the top for an unprincipled adventurer. Francis Harison was his hatchetman.

They were so close that Cosby almost made Harison chief justice following the dismissal of Lewis Morris. Delancey, who got the post, was not at all happy about it, and Colden tells us:

Mr Delancey excused his accepting of the commission at the expense of his predecessor by saying that the Governor could not be diverted from removing Mr Morris, and that if he did not accept it the Governor was resolved to put Mr Harison in the office, a man nowise acceptable to anybody. If that had been done it would certainly have been of great advantage to Mr Morris, for Mr Harison was of so bad a character, and so odious to the people, that they certainly would have pulled him from the Bench.[8]

Harison finally went too far in his shady deals and ruined himself. William Truesdale, one of the small fry who worked for him, owed a debt to a persistent creditor, Joseph Weldon of Boston. Somehow Harison got hold of a dunning letter from Weldon to Truesdale. Just what he had in mind is not clear—a pathetic lament that the historian has to make so often in dealing with what passed for ratiocination in this particular mind—but he caused a warrant to be sworn out against Truesdale in Weldon's name. If you think he simply had his minion arrested without further ado, you do not know Francis Harison. His behavior is described thus by Colden:

Mr Harison met Truesdale at an ale house where, pretending not to like the beer, he invited Truesdale and his company to meet him two hours afterwards at another house. When Truesdale came to the other house he found the Under-Sheriff, who immediately arrested him. Truesdale sends to Mr Harison, as his friend, to help him in his distress. As soon as Mr Harison came, he, in a seeming great surprise, said to Truesdale, "In the name of God, what is this? I hear you are arrested for such a sum"—and blamed him for not informing of it that he might have kept him out of the Sheriff's way.[9]

New York's archvillain must have been very pleased with himself as his victim was carted off to jail. Did he whisper, "Honest Iago!" to himself?

The roguery was there, but as usual there was no intelligence to back it up and make it work. The intriguer had counted on a smooth explanation to fend off the man in whose name he was practicing on Truesdale. Instead, Joseph Weldon felt outraged when he learned what was going on, rushed down from Boston, swore that he never gave anyone any authority to act for him, and added that at the time he did not even know of Harison's existence.

After this scandal there was no place in New York for Francis Harison. Even his protector in the governor's mansion could not save him. A Grand Jury indicted him for using Weldon's name, whereupon he fled from the Colony in May of 1735, made his way to England, and never came back. From then on his story is virtually a blank, the last word on him being that he was down-and-out when he died.

However, this melancholy denouement was in the future and unforeseen when Cosby put Harison in charge of the *Gazette* in 1732. The new editor began to ride very high indeed, for he was in the enviable position of one who could both flatter his own side and castigate its critics with impunity since there was no rival newspaper to contradict him. With Harison in command, the administration's mouthpiece lavished on William Cosby the adulation that he loved and could get only from a trusted henchman, interspersing at the same time quick jabs at Morris, Van Dam, Alexander, and the rest.

Here is the way the *Gazette* covered one meeting between the Governor and the Assembly:

The harmony and good understanding between the several branches of the legislature—whereby nothing came to be demanded on the one side but what was for the public general good and welfare of His Majesty's people, and everything done on the other which may recommend the honorable House to His Majesty, to his representative and to their constituents—will, we hope, continue to us all those blessings which we enjoy under a government greatly envied, and too often disturbed by such as, instead thereof, are struggling to introduce discord and public confusion.[10]

The *Gazette* resorted to verse to make its case:

Cosby the mild, the happy, good and great,

The strongest guard of our little state;

Let malcontents in crabbed language write,

And the D...h H...s belch, tho' they cannot bite.

He unconcerned will let the wretches roar,

And govern just, as others did before.[11]

It went to Pope's translation of the *Odyssey* to find a suitable description of the opposing faction:

Thersites only clamored in the throng,

Loquacious, loud, and turbulent of tongue,

And by no shame, by no respect controlled;

In scandal busy, in reproaches bold;

But chief, he gloried with licentious style,

To lash the great, and rulers to revile.[12]

These passages epitomize the problem facing the Popular party. In fighting the Governor there was no hope of success unless he could be met at every critical spot, and one of the most critical was precisely that of journalism. Irregular pamphlets and open letters were of little use against a systematic weekly dose of administration propaganda in the *Gazette*. The passage of time only made the problem more acute.

Naturally we do not have minutes of the discussions that went on between the anti-Cosby conspirators, but we do not need such information to see the rationale of the strategy they worked out. Their behavior is most eloquent on that score; it systematizes by practical example the disjointed notes, memoranda, and other documents that have come down to us.

First of all, they would do everything they could to sap the political strength of their hated enemy: they would support opposing candidates at elections, they would provide legal counsel for those whom he attacked through the courts, they would found a newspaper to bring their side of the controversy before the bar of public opinion. Secondly, they would wage their war on another front, in London, sending to the Board of Trade a steady barrage of propaganda designed to prove that William Cosby was no more fit to govern New York than he had been to govern Minorca. Eventually they would dispatch an emissary to make the situation clear in personal talks with the authorities.

VI. An Opposition Newspaper

With the lines thus drawn up, the first blows were struck on October 29, 1733. On that day was held the election of an assemblyman for Westchester, and the candidate of the Popular party was Lewis Morris. Governor Cosby, desperately anxious to defeat this formidable antagonist, threw everything he had to the support of his own man, William Forster. The result was the famous poll on the green of St. Paul's Church, Eastchester.[1]

The two candidates, arriving with motley arrays of their followers behind them, were like commanding generals bound for battle. The image is not at all inexact, for Westchester was a stronghold of the Delancey-Philipse element of the Court party, and both sides were able to count on a disciplined mass of voters.

The sheriff presiding over the election was, like many officials, a creature of the Governor. Cosby evidently had ordered him to make sure, in one way or another, that the result went against Morris—in other words, to rig the election if necessary. When it became clear that Morris had a majority of the voters with him, the sheriff intervened and tried to snatch a victory by disfranchising one whole body of the population.

It had been customary to let Quakers vote without taking the oath, for by their religion they were forbidden to "swear." Instead they were allowed to "affirm." That custom gave Cosby's sheriff a loophole. He decreed that no one who would not take the oath should be allowed to cast a ballot, and so he ruled the Friends out of the election, hoping that this maneuver would change the result. In fact it did not, for even without this group of his supporters Morris won a resounding victory.

The election was momentous beyond the fact that it returned to the Assembly a veteran of rough-and-tumble politics who was sure to throw his weight against the Governor wherever he could, and that it hardened the Quakers against the regime. It revealed Cosby as completely unscrupulous in dealing with his opponents, as a man who, occupying the position of chief upholder of the law, had no hesitation in playing fast and loose with it when he thought he could gain some advantage. Before the election he had been guilty of many questionable things, such as the legal attack on Van Dam and the removal of Lewis Morris from the Supreme Court, but these were at least debatable, with something to be said for him even if he could not be exculpated. Now his conduct was not debatable. It was plainly unethical, if not technically illegal.

The Westchester election was, in more ways than one, a triumph for the Popular party, which had impelled Cosby into a crime that was at once manifest and useless, revealing him as stupid as well as criminal.

The furor had hardly begun to die away before there burst upon the Governor the bombshell of an opposition newspaper. The *New York Weekly Journal,* edited by James Alexander and printed by Peter Zenger, was the first *political independent* ever published on this continent. The men behind it created a journalistic category new to American experience when they deliberately decided to make a continuing open battle with Governor Cosby the rationale of their editorial policy. They published a specifically political newspaper, no arm of the authorities or toady to headquarters, but the mouthpiece of those who were challenging the representative of the king in their Colony. There was nothing hesitant or sporadic about their undertaking. The paper came out every Monday, always truculent and always propagandizing one point of view in politics. The political issue was the only *raison d'être* of publication. Everything else—foreign news, essays, verses, squibs, advertisements—was filler.

Here was something original for this side of the ocean, an experiment in journalism as critical as ever was attempted by any members of our fourth estate; and successful, for the *Journal* lived and throve and became the ancestor of the great American political organs of modern times.

Now for all of this James Alexander was more responsible than any other man. From his literary remains we know that he was in full possession of the theory of a free press long before the occasion rose for him to implement it as a working editor, and that, the occasion having risen, he wrote much of the copy for the opposition newspaper and blue-penciled virtually all the contributions bearing on the feud with the Governor.

This pivotal figure of American history was Scottish by birth, heir to the title of Earl of Stirling (a title his son made illustrious in the patriotic annals of the Revolution). He studied mathematics and science in Edinburgh, but compromised his future there by joining the Jacobite rising that attempted to place the Old Pretender on the British throne in 1715. After the fiasco, Alexander, like so many of his class, found Scotland too hot for him. He fled to America, studied law, went into politics, and eventually entered the Councils of both New York and New Jersey. Mathematician, scientist, lawyer, and politician, he was one of the most extraordinary men of his generation, a gentleman and a scholar, a charter member of Benjamin Franklin's Philosophical Society, and the trusted confidant of more than one Governor.

The idea of founding the *Journal* was probably his. For one thing, he was already something of a journalist, having published various items in William Bradford's *Gazette* when it was the only newspaper in town. Secondly, he was among the first overt opponents of Governor Cosby, the collision between them being remarkably quick and remarkably bitter, perhaps even more so than the Cosby-Morris and the Cosby-Van Dam conflicts. Only a few months after arriving the Governor wrote to his patron, the Duke of Newcastle:

There is one, James Alexander, whom I found here in both the New York and the New Jersey Councils, although very unfit to sit in either, or indeed to act in any other capacity where His Majesty's honor and interest are concerned. He is the only man that has given me any uneasiness since my arrival.... In short, his known very bad character would be too long to trouble Your Grace with particulars, and stuffed with such tricks and oppressions too gross for Your Grace to hear. In his room I desire the favor of Your Grace to appoint Joseph Warrell.[13]

Many more letters of a similar content passed between the governor's mansion in New York and authoritative personages in England.

Alexander repaid the compliment in his own correspondence. To his old friend, former Governor Robert Hunter, he confided:

Our Governor, who came here but last year, has long ago given more distaste to the people than I believe any Governor that ever this Province had during his whole government. He was so unhappy before he came to have the character in England that he knew not the difference between power and right; and he has, by many imprudent actions since he came here, fully verified that character. It would be tedious to give a detail of them. He has raised such a spirit in the people of this Province that, if they cannot convince him, yet I believe they will give the world reason to believe that they are not easily to be made slaves of, nor to be governed by arbitrary power.... Nothing does give a greater luster to your and Mr Burnet's administrations here than being succeeded by such a man.[14]

This letter is notable for giving Alexander's own express statement about the reason for publishing the brand new *Journal*:

Inclosed is also the first of a newspaper designed to be continued weekly, chiefly to expose him [Cosby] and those ridiculous flatteries with which Mr Harison loads our other newspaper, which our Governor claims and has the privilege of suffering nothing to be in but what he and Mr Harison approve of.

Mr Van Dam is resolved, and by far the greater part of the Province openly approve his resolution, of not yielding to the Governor's demand. He has not as yet answered, nor will the Governor's lawyers be able for one while to compel him unless they break over all law and persuade the new Judges [Delancey and Philipse] into a contradiction of themselves. Which if they do, the world shall know it from the press.[15]

The advent of the *Journal* did nothing to lessen the bitterness of Cosby's condemnation of Alexander, for although it was known as "Zenger's paper" (since it bore only the printer's name), the Governor was in no doubt about who was the guiding genius of the enterprise. On December 6, 1734, he writes to the Board of Trade:

Mr James Alexander is the person whom I have too much occasion to mention.... No sooner did Van Dam and the late Chief Justice (the latter especially) begin to treat my administration with rudeness and ill-manners than I found Alexander to be at the head of a scheme to give all imaginable uneasiness to the government by infusing into, and making the worst impression on, the minds of the people. A press supported by him and his party began to swarm with the most virulent libels.[16]

Cosby realized further that Alexander was not the only one in New York who was playing at the new kind of journalism, and he said of Morris:

His open and implacable malice against me has appeared weekly in Zenger's *Journal*. This man with the two others I have mentioned, Van Dam and Alexander, are the only men from whom I am to look for any opposition in the administration of the government, and they are so implacable in their malice that I am to look for all the insolent, false and scandalous aspersions that such bold and profligate wretches can invent.[17]

Cosby's cries of rage and anguish are understandable enough. From the date of the *Journal*'s appearance (November 5, 1733) until his death more than two years later it constituted itself his most alert censor, critic, and judge. Every Monday the lash fell across his shoulders, the attacks varying through the gamut from airy satire to thundering condemnation. The opposition writers called him everything from an "idiot" to a "Nero," and pointedly suggested that his London superiors should do something to alleviate the affliction they had imposed on their Colony.

The first issue started the ball rolling with a brilliant and biting story of the Westchester election and Morris' victory in spite of the sheriff's heavy-handed machinations; and from then on there was no letup. The fundamental idea being to convict Cosby of violating the rules of his governorship, the *Journal* never ceased to hammer at this theme. The best example of the technique is in the issues of the last two weeks of September, 1734, a continued essay that accuses Cosby of voting as a member of the Council during its legislative sessions, of demanding that bills from the Assembly be presented to him before the Council saw them, and of adjourning the Assembly in his own name instead of the king's.

All three of these acts violated the rules by which the Governor was bound, and when the *Journal* carried the story to the Board of Trade, Cosby was warned about them. He could not, of course, be condemned out of hand on the basis of a newspaper story, but the significant thing is that the Board should have found the story sufficient basis for mentioning the subject.

Most of the *Journal* writing is lost irretrievably behind a veil of anonymity, which is not too important since whoever "Cato" and "Philo-Patriae" and "Thomas Standby" may have been, they were acting in concert. But every once in a while individual personality peeps or glares through the writing, as in this reply to one argument for the prudence of obeying the government, no matter what. The text of the reply is saturated through and through with the pent-up gall and venom on which Lewis Morris had been feeding for so long:

Let this wiseacre (whoever he is) go to any country wife and tell her that the fox is a mischievous creature that can and does do her much hurt, that it is difficult if not impracticable to catch him, and that therefore she ought on any terms to keep in with him.

Why don't we keep in with serpents and wolves on this foot? Animals much more innocent and less mischievous to the public than some Governors have proved.

A Governor turns rogue, does a thousand things for which a small rogue would have deserved a halter; and because it is difficult if not impracticable to obtain relief against him, therefore it is prudent to keep in with him and join in the roguery; and that on the principle of self-preservation. That is, a Governor does all he can to chain you, and it being difficult to prevent him, it is prudent in you (in order to preserve your liberty) to help him put them on and to rivet them fast.

No people in the world have contended for liberty with more boldness and greater success than the Dutch; are more tenacious in retaining it; or more jealous of any attempts upon it; yet in their plantations they seem to be lost to all the sense of it, and a fellow that is but one degree removed from an idiot shall, with a full-mouthed "Sacrament, Donder and Blixum!" govern as he pleases, dispose of them and their properties at his discretion, and their magistrates will keep in with him at any rate, and think his favor no mean purchase for the loss of their liberty.

There have been Nicholsons, Cornburys, Coots, Barringtons, Edens, Lowthers, Georges, Parks, Douglases, and many more, as very Bashaws as ever were sent out from Constantinople; and there have not been wanting under each of their administrations persons, the dregs and scandals of human nature, who have kept in with them and used their endeavors to enslave their fellow-subjects, and persuaded others to do so.[18]

> This was political independence with a vengeance. Never before had an American newspaper dared to treat an officer of the crown so. Other periodicals depended on official sanction to keep them going, or at least never strayed too far from the line laid down for them. The *Journal* had no sanction and toed no line. It was, depending on one's political sympathies, either an outrageous innovation or else simply an unfamiliar experiment. In either case it needed to be legitimized in the eyes of its readers.

VII. Freedom of the Press

That was why Alexander, as editor, pushed the issue of freedom of the press so hard. New Yorkers who had been unaware of that freedom would come upon it every time they opened "Zenger's paper." Side by side they would find stories about the misdemeanors of the Governor and essays defending and defining a free press, an ingenious interplay of practice and theory, a journalistic dialectic shifting between independent news reporting and the theory that justifies such reporting. Under Alexander's editing hand the contributors both pilloried their enemy in the executive mansion and claimed the right to do so.

Alexander did not, of course, invent the technique. It was already well known in Britain, and he took it over for his own purposes, just as our political philosophers such as Jefferson, Franklin, and Madison took over ideas already current in Britain and France. Like all our Colonial editors, he was dependent on classics such as Milton, Locke, Swift, Steele, Addison, and Defoe. He used all of these at different times, quoting them as authorities for unfettered journalism and free speech.

Most of all he used the celebrated *Cato's Letters* of Thomas Gordon and John Trenchard. They furnished him with an ideal model. The letters had appeared in the *London Journal* and the *British Journal* only a decade before, when, signing themselves "Cato," Gordon and Trenchard castigated his majesty's government, and particularly the men responsible for the scandal of the South Sea Bubble. They also larded their attacks with animadversions on freedom of the press, which they explicitly defended as intrinsic to liberty itself. They caused so much embarrassment to the Ministry that it was forced to counterattack: characteristically for the eighteenth century, it solved the problem by buying out the *London Journal.*

But that did not kill the argument, for *Cato's Letters* were published in four volumes and enjoyed a tremendous popularity on both sides of the Atlantic. It took James Alexander to show just how much might be done with them over here. He manifestly had read and reread Gordon and Trenchard, soaking up their ideas as avidly as a sponge soaks up water, and, turning editor, he found in them a treasure trove of journalistic philosophy and invective. His policy is theirs adapted to the situation in Colonial New York.

He copied out extracts from the *Letters* both for his own private edification and guidance and for use in the *Journal.* There is extant in his handwriting part of the letter headed "Of the restraints which ought to be laid upon public rulers." He thought it apropos of the Cosby administration, so it appeared in the *Journal* on May 27, 1734. Here are a few others that he selected, or else approved, for reprinting: "The right and capacity of the people to judge of government," "Of reverence true and false," "Of freedom of speech: that the same is inseparable from public liberty," "Reflections upon libelling," "Cautions against the natural encroachments of power."

To put his editorial credo in a nutshell, Alexander went to another classical source, the *Craftsman*, and printed this maxim on November 12, 1733:

The liberty of the press is a subject of the greatest importance, and in which every individual is as much concerned as he is in any other part of liberty.

Under the aegis of his text he adroitly maneuvered the opposition newspaper against all the power of the Governor—and against all the defenses thrown up by Francis Harison as editor of the Governor's newspaper.

VIII. A Newspaper War

The *Journal*'s anti-Cosby campaign touched off the first of the many newspaper wars that have raged on the banks of the Hudson. As often as it attacked did the *Gazette* rush to the rescue amid an acrimonious exchange of accusations and insults. Thus, referring to the sentiments of the people of New York toward their Governor:

The *Journal*. They think, as matters now stand, that their liberties and properties are precarious, and that slavery is like to be entailed on them and their posterity if some past things be not amended.[19]

The *Gazette*. Now give me leave to say what I have reason to believe some of the people of this City and Province think in relation to that paragraph in Zenger's paper. They think it is an aggravated libel.[20]

In such a tone did New York's two newspapers carry on their duel, one which concedes nothing to the later age of yellow journalism in its furious charges and countercharges of deceit, ignorance, calumny, and slander. The above onset and riposte stand out because the passage from the *Journal* sounds like Alexander himself, while Governor Cosby agreed with the *Gazette* that it was "libelous" and made it part of the formal indictment of Peter Zenger.

Both sides went at it hammer and tongs. In the *Journal*, where Cosby is called a "Nero," his kept journalist is his "spaniel." The *Gazette* retorts with epithets like "seditious rogues" and "disaffected instigators of arson and riot," and proposes that the name "Zenger" be turned into a common-noun synonym for "liar."

The men behind the opposition newspaper made a point of referring to Harison obliquely in satirical mock "advertisements" like these:

A large spaniel of about five foot five inches high has lately strayed from his kennel with his mouth full of fulsome panegyrics, and in his ramble dropped them in the *New York Gazette*. When a puppy he was marked thus (FH), and a cross in the middle of his forehead; but the mark being worn out, he has taken upon him in a heathenish manner to abuse mankind by imposing a great many gross falsehoods on them. Whoever will strip the said panegyrics of their fulsomeness, and send the beast back to his kennel, shall have the thanks of all honest men, and all reasonable charges.[21]

The spaniel strayed away is of his own accord returned to his kennel, from whence he begs leave to assure the public that all those fulsome panegyrics were dropped in the *New York Gazette* by the express orders of his master; and that for the gross falsehoods he is charged with imposing upon mankind, he is willing to undergo any punishment the people will impose on him if they can make full proof in any Court of Record that any one individual person in the Province (that knew him) believed any of them.[22]

The writers of these squibs had measured their man perfectly. They could become furious, caustic, ironic or insulting—that is, *serious*—with the Governor and the rest of the men around him; but the proper approach to Francis Harison was through satire. From the *Journal* he received a systematic dose of it.

For six months he absorbed the barbs of ridicule while maintaining an air of indifference. Finally, able to stand the badgering no longer, he whirled on his tormentors and attempted to repay them in their own coin:

Supposing another should turn the tables upon the authors of these infamous and fictitious advertisements, how easily might it be done? The real or imagined defects of the *Amsterdam Crane*, the *Connecticut Mastiff, Phillip Baboon, Senior, Phillip Baboon, Junior*, the *Scythian Unicorn*, and *Wild Peter from the Banks of the Rhine* might be enlarged upon, and placed in a most ludicrous light.[23]

Since the crass and clumsy Harison was devoid of the slightest capacity for satire, he inevitably suffered when he picked up the weapon that was wielded so devastatingly by his enemies. The only interesting thing about this paragraph is that it identifies the men of the Popular party who contributed most to the *Journal*: Rip Van Dam, William Smith, Lewis Morris, Senior, Lewis Morris, Junior, James Alexander, and Peter Zenger.

The honors of combat obviously went to "Zenger's paper." It was not always fair, by a long shot—nor has any newspaper ever been when fighting a war with a rival. But Cosby and Harison and the Court party *in toto* were too vulnerable for all the *Journal's* broadsides to go astray. The Governor was hit over and over again. So was his editor. So were his other cronies.

They fought back in the *Gazette*, but they were always on the defensive, always incapable of getting a real attack going. Finally Cosby, boiling with rage, determined on something more practical than a war of words.

IX. Zenger Goes to Jail

The Governor paused long enough to see what could be done through the usual legal channels, with Chief Justice Delancey given the job of extracting a grand jury indictment for libel. That this attempt failed twice is indicative of the administration's unpopularity. The jurors manifestly had determined from the start that they would do nothing, and though they were in no more doubt than Delancey about the identity of the principal men who wrote for the *Journal*, they used the "anonymity" of the affair as an excuse to avoid indicting anybody.

With the second grand jury failure, Cosby's attention began to focus more intently on the newspaper and its printer. His next move was to order copies of the obnoxious periodical to be burned, which was done even though the Assembly and the magistrates refused to participate. Naturally the man in charge was the man maintained expressly for such purposes. Harison was all the more eager to perform the duty in that, besides the eternal ridicule the *Journal* heaped on him, in one issue it had run a letter from the freeholders of Orange County thanking their assemblyman, Vincent Matthews, for making a vitriolic attack on him from the floor of the legislature. A copy from that issue was one of four earmarked for the flames.

The hatchetman's first instinct was to adopt strong-arm methods. He therefore went around to Peter Zenger's establishment, disburdened himself of some violent opinions ("more fit to be uttered by a drayman than a gentleman," says Peter), and threatened to cane him on the street. That was why the printer took to wearing a sword whenever he went out—the sword that gave an excuse for much heavy sarcasm in the columns of the *Gazette*.

Harison did not overlook more indirect and devious methods of dealing with his critics. He sent a couple of his creatures, John Alsop and Edward Blagg, to Orange County to spread the story that the *Journal* with the freeholders' letter commending Matthews had been burned by the common hangman, and that the signers were to be rounded up and thrown into jail—a rumor that caused some trepidation among the solid citizens of the county.

Unfortunately Harison, misjudging the situation in his usual fashion, had jumped the gun a little too smartly. He counted on the hangman to do the job because he himself, as recorder of New York City, was supposed to persuade the magistrates to throw their authority behind the ceremonial burning. But when he met with them, he found himself in an atmosphere of chilly distrust, for they knew that Cosby was trying to kill legitimate opposition. Harison started to argue that there were sound British precedents for dealing thus with the *Journal*; was quickly shown up as grossly ignorant on that score (he put up the defense that he did not carry his lawbooks around with him); was roundly snubbed; and departed in a spasm of fury. The magistrates then forbade anyone within their authority, including the hangman, to have anything to do with the affair.

The *Journal* was burned on schedule, with Harison presiding, but he had to bring in a slave to set the fire, and they were virtually alone in front of the City Hall as the flames rose. It was the most dismal fiasco of a career studded with fiascoes.

We can judge how heated the situation had become by reverting once more to that most percipient of contemporary witnesses, Cadwallader Colden:

One might think, after such aversion to this prosecution appeared from all sorts of people, that it would have been thought prudent to have desisted from farther proceedings. But the violent resentment of many in the administration who had been exposed in Zenger's papers, together with the advantage they thought of gaining by his papers being found libels by a Jury, blinded their eyes so that they did not see what any man of common understanding would here have seen, and did see.[24]

Governor Cosby was indeed blind. He was blinded by a baffled fury that had grown increasingly unreasoning as his hopes crumbled into nothingness. Instead of bowing to his will, his enemies were causing him grave embarrassment with his superiors, compelling him to a perpetual defense of his right to remain in his office. And locally they had made him a laughingstock. With cool impudence Morris and Alexander (these two above any) tormented him from behind the safeguard of an "anonymity" that fooled nobody, and was intended to fool nobody—least of all the victim of their attacks, for the dagger was honed to a fine edge precisely by Cosby's awareness of who held it. The commanders of the Popular party were all very much at large, hurling their invectives at him and satirizing his attempts to retaliate.

The hunters had fenced in the tiger, and were baiting him from a safe distance, prodding him into a frenzy—until with a single bound he leaped on the one man who stood within reach.

Printer Peter Zenger had not even a specious "anonymity" between him and the Governor. The *Journal* was "his" newspaper. Accordingly a warrant for his arrest went out from the Governor and the Council, and the sheriff arrested Zenger on November 17, 1734, and held him for trial on a charge of "seditious libel." Harison, needless to say, was one of the councillors who signed the warrant; in fact, he is the only person mentioned by name as having done so in the well-known "apology" that Zenger printed in his newspaper on November 25:

As you last week were disappointed of my *Journal*, I think it incumbent on me to publish my apology, which is this. On the Lord's Day, the seventeenth, I was arrested, taken and imprisoned in the common jail of this City by virtue of a warrant from the Governor, the honorable Francis Harison, and others in the Council (of which, God willing, you will have a copy); whereupon I was put under such restraint that I had not the liberty of pen, ink or paper, or to see or speak with people, until upon my complaint to the honorable Chief Justice at my appearing before him upon my habeas corpus on the Wednesday following. He discountenanced that proceeding, and therefore I have had since that time the liberty of speaking thro' the hole of the door to my wife and servants. By which I doubt not you will think me sufficiently excused for not sending my last week's *Journal*, and hope for the future, by the liberty of speaking to my servants thro' the hole of the door of the prison, to entertain you with my weekly *Journal* as formerly.

During all the printer's imprisonment the *Journal* failed of but that one issue. The credit for its punctual appearance every Monday thereafter belongs to his wife, Anna Catherine Zenger, who stepped into his shoes back at the shop. Anna Catherine has a real claim to fame for standing by her husband, a loyalty by no means insignificant in a woman with a family. She may have been emboldened by her ability to keep the press going in his absence, but even so it would have been a crushing blow if he had been given a harsh sentence as, for all she knew, might have been the outcome. The little evidence there is indicates that she never pressed him to give in and name the men who actually were responsible for the *Journal*. She must have known that the New York administration would gladly trade the printer for the editor, a comparatively minor figure for the archenemy—that is, Peter Zenger for James Alexander—but there is no record of her ever complaining that the Zenger family was suffering for someone else.

The Court party's editor used the occasion for a show of mock sympathy with the Popular party's printer. The *Gazette* for December 9, 1734, has a reference to

the pretended patriots of our days, the correspondents of John Peter Zenger, who are every hour undermining the credit and authority of the government by all the wicked methods and low artifices that can be devised, and which they flatter themselves are consistent with their own safety. I am sorry they are so tenacious of their own as to neglect that of their poor printer.

Harison had a fine time thinking up jibes like this. It would have been poetic justice if he had been around to suffer—with Governor Cosby and the rest of the Court party—through the acquittal Peter Zenger won so triumphantly on August 4, 1735. But by that time New York had become too hot for this particular member of the faction, and he was on the other side of the Atlantic.

The arrest of Peter Zenger was one of Cosby's gross mistakes. No one in the Colony could miss the fact that he was bent on revenge, for the public bodies—Assembly, Common Council, grand juries—had all refused to have anything to do with proceedings that they recognized as strictly the Governor's private affair. Nor could there be any doubt that his purpose was to silence a critic who had been uttering unpalatable truths. Popular feeling was exacerbated by the fact that Cosby's vindictive wrath fell, not upon the powerful men of the opposite faction, but upon an insignificant German immigrant who plied the trade of printer in the city.

The way the thing was done added to the animosity that Cosby provoked. Zenger's bail was placed at so high a figure that he could not meet it, his lawyers were disbarred for protesting against the Governor's hand-picked court of Chief Justice James Delancey and Associate Justice Frederick Philipse, the prisoner had to linger in his cell for nine months before he was given his day in court, and Cosby tried for a packed jury in so blatant a way that his own chief justice had to disavow him. None of this could be kept secret; when the trial was finally held local sentiment had turned against the Governor to the point where he had only his closest friends with him.

X. Van Dam's Indictment of the Governor

As the Zenger case developed step by step in New York, Cosby was being forced to a more energetic defense on the London front, where Van Dam was waging a pamphlet war against him, and where Morris was present in person.

Months before the newspaper war began Van Dam had resolved to keep the New York public and the London authorities informed of the way in which the Cosby suit for half of his salary was going, and he began to publish successive accounts, with Peter Zenger doing the printing for him just as for the rest of the Popular party. Zenger's business got better as the political controversy got worse. In the summer of 1733 he turned out for Alexander and Smith their arguments against the validity of the equity court. Shortly afterward Van Dam gave him the job of handling two protests in which the stubborn old Dutchman expressed his personal indignation at the way he was being treated by the Governor.

These partial attacks on Cosby were followed by a general indictment, a full bill of particulars drawn up to expose him point by point with the most meticulous exactitude. Almost everything that could be alleged against him with any degree of plausibility at all was set down in Van Dam's *Articles of Complaint*.

The apparent author was not the real one. Van Dam undoubtedly had a hand in formulating the charges, but the writing must have been due to someone else since Van Dam was not skillful with the pen. James Alexander springs to mind as the obvious candidate for the role of ghost writer, a suspicion that is strengthened by the accusations that Cosby leveled at both him and Morris. Nevertheless, Van Dam was responsible for the *Articles*, a fact on which he insisted with dogged self-righteousness.

The indictment is composed of 34 separate counts. Not all of them are watertight, for some descend into carping criticism about trivialities. One, for instance, accuses Cosby of accepting a gift of French wines from the commander at Louisbourg:

You received of the said Frenchman by way of present all of the said brandy, claret and salad oil, which were carried into the fort and lodged in your cellar; and this, I suppose, induced you to grant a liberty to trade here, which you ought not to have done.[25]

Another charges that Cosby's candidate in the Westchester election, William Forster, was "a known Jacobite," an astonishing grievance in this context since James Alexander was himself a Jacobite, a veteran of the rising of 1715.

These are mere debaters' points (at the most charitable estimation), and they prove that the leaders of the Popular party could be just as unscrupulous as the Governor when they put their minds to it. They did not disdain to use against him the weapons that he used against them. Too often the struggle has been painted in stark tones of black and white, when it was really a matter of degree, with neither side having a monopoly of either vice or virtue—which is to say little more than that we are dealing with the factional politics of real men rather than with the stereotypes of melodrama.

Again, some of the *Articles* are of doubtful validity, as when Cosby is accused of destroying a deed given to the City of Albany by the Mohawks, and of permitting the French to map and sound New York harbor on the pretence of trading there. The Governor retorted that the deed was unjust to begin with, and that to have kept it in force would have driven the Indians into the arms of the French; and that trade with Louisbourg was legitimate and humanitarian because the garrison was close to famine.

But if a number of the *Articles* have a dubious ring, others do make fundamental points. They mention the dismissal of Morris from the Supreme Court, the Van Dam lawsuit, and the attempt to rig the Westchester election. Several are devoted to Cosby's contemptuous treatment of his Council:

You have, contrary to your instructions, displaced Judges, Justices of the Peace, Sheriffs, etc., without the advice of Council.[26]

The Council being part of the legislature, as above, you have taken it upon you (in order to influence their debates) to sit among them and act as their President, though by your patent His Majesty has given you a negative voice to prevent the passing of any law prejudicial to His Majesty's prerogative and the public good.[27]

Where the advice of the Council has been thought necessary you have not given general summonses as usual, but have only summoned so small a number as would constitute a quorum, in which you were sure of a majority to carry such point as you thought proper, and by this method seem to support your proceedings by the sanction of advice of Council—when three makes a majority of such a quorum, and nine might have been dissenting had they been summoned.[28]

You have taken it upon yourself to act as President of the Council in receiving bills and messages from the General Assembly.[29]

By these methods you have rendered the Council useless in their legislative capacity of being that check and balance in government that His Majesty intended they should be.[30]

> Van Dam's *Articles of Complaint* constituted a deadly blow at Governor Cosby, what with his Minorca past added to his present troubles in New York, nor was he slow to recognize the fact. We have already seen how he was warned by the Board of Trade because of reports in the *Journal*. Fearing the effect of the *Articles* in London, he prompted his confederates of the Council to draw up for the Duke of Newcastle a point by point "refutation"— which does not, however, actually refute anything fundamental, for if it deals validly enough with the trivialities, it sedulously avoids, or else boldly denies, the facts about Cosby's maladministration and misdemeanors. At the same time the Cosby councillors appended a note that gives the Court party's version of the New York situation:

We have been, while we traced Mr Van Dam through a labyrinth of detestable falsehoods, very often at a loss how to believe that a man of his years could forge so many and so notorious scandals, but we are to inform your Grace that the resentment, malice and revenge of some of the wickedest men are thrown to his assistance. No government or administration can please these restless minds. Nothing will satisfy them but the power which they joyfully would exercise to the destruction or ruin of their fellow subjects. We beg

Your Lordship to be assured that we know, and daily are made more sensible of, our happiness under His Excellency's administration.[31]

XI. Morris on the London Front

During the year 1734 the quarrel between Governor Cosby and his enemies went on, and then in December he learned that Lewis Morris had sailed for England. Things were becoming more tense. The two factions had met head-on in another election contest, that for the Common Council of New York City, and again the Governor had suffered a humiliating defeat. Smarting with resentment, and goaded by mounting fury, he had promptly turned around and thrown himself on the one man who was vulnerable: he had jailed Peter Zenger on the charge of "seditious libel." If the printer should be convicted, that alone would justify Cosby, and compromise his opponents, in the eyes of the authorities. The leaders of the Zenger faction might join their printer in the city prison. At best, the opposition press would be muzzled, in which case the anti-Cosbyites would have to go outside New York to have their pamphlets printed, while their newspaper must be destroyed.

There was no time to lose. The plan to send a personal representative to London should be implemented, Lewis Morris being a satisfactory choice since he was already known in the British capital. Everything was done as secretly as possible, and Morris embarked clandestinely to prevent the Governor's taking any countermeasures.

The strategy for him to follow had been worked out in consultations with his colleagues. We know the generalities of the case he was to make against the Cosby administration, and they are of special interest as indicating how the Popular party thought London should be approached. Here we find no trivialities such as those in the *Articles of Complaint*. Morris was to adhere strictly to criticisms that told:

At a consultation between James Alexander, William Smith, and Lewis Morris Jun., as to the matters to be entrusted to Col. M—, it was determined that he should exert himself to procure among other things: The removal of the Governor if possible—his own restoration [to the Supreme Court]—the dissolution of the then existing Assembly—the removal of Francis Harison and Daniel Horsmanden from the Council of New York—instructions to Gov. Cosby to pass such laws as a new Assembly should conceive conducive to the welfare of the people, and particularly an act for an annual or triennial Assembly, and some others of a special character—to allow the Council to sit without him, and that their advice and consent should be required in conformity with his instructions—that the Governor should also be instructed not to set himself above the law—to grant new charters to the cities of New York and Albany—and that only by adhering to these directions could he hope to be retained in office.[32]

> Morris followed his instructions as well, apparently, as he could during almost two years in England. He was quickly disillusioned about the possibility of getting what he wanted. Being of a choleric and impetuous nature, he may have pressed his demands too warmly and eagerly; he may have been too obviously the partisan. But one reason why the recall of Cosby could not be achieved was that too many interests in London wanted him to stay where he was. In a letter to Alexander, Morris wrote:

Everybody here agrees in a contemptible opinion of Cosby, and nobody knows him better, or has a worse opinion of him, than the friends he relies on; and it may be you will be surprised to hear that the most nefarious crime a Governor can commit is not by some counted so bad as the crime of complaining of it—the last is an arraigning of the Ministry that advised the sending of him.[33]

> In order to placate Morris, it was suggested to him that he withdraw his indictment of Cosby in return for a promise that he himself should be appointed the first governor of New Jersey under a separate jurisdiction. He announced publicly his refusal of the offer (although some murmuring about his candor was heard when he received that office in 1738). On one point he was partially successful, that of his removal from the Supreme Court: a royal decree declared the reasons for it insufficient. But even so he was not reinstated. His mission to London was not a success. Perhaps the authorities, not at all enthusiastic about removing a governor to begin with, were swayed by Cosby's accusations against Morris, such as:

Cabals were formed against the government, and a meeting of their factious men is still held several nights in the week at a private lodging which I have discovered, Alexander always present, and Morris, till he lately fled privately for England, in great fear as 'tis publicly reported lest the printer of their seditious libels should discover him.[34]

> The Governor certainly had some success with his London defense. He was, after all, the crown's executive on the spot, and that alone would have given his pronouncements an authority denied to the greatest magnates of the Popular party. The burden of proof lay with them. That they thought they could meet the

test is proved by the commission given to Lewis Morris. But, if the Board of Trade went so far as to censure Cosby, they obviously felt inclined to accept his version of what was going on in New York. To the Queen they reported:

Colonel Cosby acquaints us in his letter that the said Alexander and his party have set up a printing press at New York, where the most virulent libels and most abusive pamphlets published against the Ministry and other persons of honor in England have been reprinted, with such alterations as served to inflame the people against the several branches of the legislature and the administration in that Province.

That factious cabals are secretly held several times a week in New York, at which Alexander is always present, as Morris was before his coming privately to England....

Colonel Cosby further acquaints us that Rip Van Dam, Morris, Alexander, and others of their party, appear by their behavior to be disaffected to his Majesty's government, and are daily exciting the people to sedition and riot.[35]

> This passage, written while Lewis Morris was there to agitate for the contrary, comes close to a real endorsement of Governor Cosby.

XII. Cosby's Defeat

Ironically, it was drawn up just a few weeks after the Governor had been condemned in New York—condemned explicitly on the score of the printing press about which he fulminated to the Board of Trade.

The trial of the printer was the critical moment for all concerned, the leaders of both sides being as anxious about the outcome as was Peter Zenger himself. Cosby had done everything he could to ensure a verdict in his favor. The defense countered by bringing in the leading attorney of Philadelphia, perhaps of the colonies, Andrew Hamilton. The common people of the city thronged the galleries as the proceedings began.

What happened during that momentous August day is one of the moving, triumphant pages of American history. We can still feel, in reading the text of the trial, the emotional tremor that vibrated in the courtroom at the clash of two powerful forces. We can still follow Andrew Hamilton as he stalks his opponents like an implacable duelist with a rapier, pinking now one and now the other as they venture to challenge him. We can understand the hot befuddlement of Chief Justice Delancey and Attorney General Bradley when they found their prepared defenses useless against a kind of attack they never expected; we can understand their moral disintegration when the verdict went against them, and they had to think what to say when they reported to the governor's mansion. How must they have felt when the crowd began a delirious demonstration to show its delight that Peter Zenger was a free man? How must they have felt, a few hours later, when they heard that Andrew Hamilton was being treated like a hero by the magistrates of the city?

Governor Cosby had suffered a crushing rebuke. His sword had turned into a boomerang. Having confidently looked for an end to the obnoxious newspaper, he found it justified in the most complete and unanswerable way—by the judgment of a group of men typical of those he governed. No longer was there any hope of silencing his critics, or of arguing with any kind of plausibility that they were guilty of seditious libel. His defense was shattered on both fronts, for New York was sure to have a moral for London. The trial he forced with such demanding arrogance undermined him, and a modest German printer became the symbol of his catastrophe—something the great Lewis Morris had been unable to engineer in face-to-face conferences with the British authorities.

The verdict seems to have broken Cosby's will. Already a sick man, suffering from pneumonia, he made no attempt to rouse himself for a renewal of the battle that had gone on from the beginning of his administration. He had never collected the salary from Van Dam, he had lost the critical elections, Alexander was still unpunished, Peter Zenger was beyond his reach, and a free press was definitely established in New York. Cosby was defeated, and he knew it.

He did strike one last blow at the old enemy who had started the trouble: he suspended Rip Van Dam from the Council. Characteristically, the obstinate Dutchman refused to acknowledge the suspension, and challenged George Clarke, the next ranking member of the Council (and a Cosby man), for the executive power in New York.

William Cosby was, appropriately enough, the prime mover in the quarrel, but this time he was not personally involved, for he died—a discredited man, but still Governor of New York—on March 10, 1736.

XIII. Andrew Hamilton

The lawyer who won the acquittal for Peter Zenger was, like his friend James Alexander, a Scot. The year of Andrew Hamilton's birth is a matter of some debate, an old story holding that he was in his eighties when he appeared in the New York courtroom, while later evidence makes him around 65 at that time. His life holds other mysteries. For one thing, we do not know why he left Scotland. It has been said that he was forced to flee after fighting a duel; again, the motive has been called political, which prompts the surmise that he was implicated in the 1715 Jacobite rising—a pleasing theory in that it allows us to imagine him and Alexander together on the same Scottish battlefield with no presentiment that their place in history lay twenty years ahead and three thousand miles away. We have too little evidence about this phase of Hamilton's life to speak authoritatively about it.

There is even some doubt that he belonged to the Hamilton clan. When he arrived in America he went by the name of Trent. However, trouble back home would account for the pseudonym, and before long he reverted to Hamilton. Rivaling Alexander in the versatility of his talents, he rose to power as soon as opportunity beckoned. He married an affluent widow, founded a great landed estate in Maryland ("Henberry," near Chestertown), went back to England to study law as a member of Gray's Inn, and then entered Colonial politics to begin an illustrious career crowned by his appointment to the Council and his election to the Assembly of Pennsylvania.

From then on his name appears prominently in Pennsylvania business. He handled legal cases for the Penn family and helped draw up addresses to the crown. He gained a reputation for opposing arbitrary acts by the Governor, especially with reference to the courts, which put him right at home when he entered the Zenger trial.

Hamilton's commanding personality had no little share in winning an acquittal for Peter Zenger. Knowing that Chief Justice Delancey would instruct the jury to leave the verdict to the court, Hamilton had to maneuver them in such a way as to make them see that they ought to ignore the instruction; and that required not only basic legal argumentation, an assured manipulation of both fact and logic, but also his own domination of the proceedings. His success was due to his courtroom presence added to his maintenance of the initiative from beginning to end. He could not afford to falter, nor did he.

By comparison, James Delancey looked like a tyro, which indeed he was—a young man, just 32, who moreover had gained his office under dubious circumstances, facing one whom he knew by reputation to be *the* old master of their common profession. Reading between the lines of the trial we are compelled to infer that Delancey lost control partly because of his own inadequacy, and partly because his hostility toward Hamilton was tempered by a deferential respect due to superior knowledge, experience, ability, and prestige. It is just as easy to see how the spectacle of the Hamilton-Delancey duel swayed the jury, prompting them to act on the advice of the defense attorney rather than on the instruction of the chief justice.

Aside from this historic victory, Hamilton is memorable as the architect of Independence Hall in Philadelphia. When the Pennsylvania Assembly decided that it needed a new building, Hamilton was named as one of the Commission to look into the problem. He submitted a plan for site and structure, had it approved by the legislators, and then supervised the work. The result was the State House in which the Assembly met for the first time in 1736. It still stands, one of the most hallowed buildings in America; now it is known from its place in the Revolution as Independence Hall.

The Zenger verdict and Independence Hall—how many men in the history of America have two comparable monuments to their memory? Andrew Hamilton had done well the two major tasks entrusted to him when he died on August 4, 1741, exactly six years to the day after the trial of Peter Zenger.

2. The Meaning of the Trial

The trial of John Peter Zenger was one of the spectacular events of American history, involving as it did powerful personalities, factional intrigue, a newspaper war, and a splendid courtroom scene in which low chicanery mingled with high rhetoric. It boasted a shining hero and a glowering villain. It passed through the dramatic sequence of conflict, climax, and denouement. It had a happy ending.

Offhand you might think that the Zenger case could be nothing more than that—a scintillating drama with a story-book finish, a tale worth telling without sequel or epilogue. Yet it was one of the most significant things that ever happened on this side of the Atlantic. It was a center from which forces—legal, political, social, constitutional—radiated throughout America, and from one generation to another down to our own time.

The historian and the dramatist may rejoice at the event as such, but the real importance of that trial of August 4, 1735, lies in what came out of it. When Peter Zenger returned to his home instead of to his prison cell, that very fact made him forever a focal point in the development and philosophy of American democracy. The implications for the future were more fundamental, varied, and far-reaching than any of the men concerned could have dreamed. It is the implications that lift the Zenger case out of the class of ordinary political prosecutions and give it a transcendent meaning.

The trial was the first, and the most important, step toward freedom of the press in America. Peter Zenger was accused of seditious libel simply because his press had turned out, and was still turning out as he stood in the dock, a newspaper with the impudence to criticize the Governor and his administration. The *New York Weekly Journal* was an astonishing spectacle in the Colonies—a periodical that preached freedom of the press as a fundamental right, and practiced its doctrine by reporting the news as it saw fit.

Other newspapers might clear their material with the authorities, or at least hedge in saying anything that could cause unpleasant repercussions. The *Journal* displayed no such self-restraint. It dwelt on the Governor's misdemeanors, alleged his incompetence, laughed at his mistakes, spotlighted his attempts to cover up his shady dealings, and more than suggested that he should be removed from office.

The *Journal* overtly and even clamorously threw off subservience to the Colonial government. It followed the lead of the British papers that had already begun the battle for a free press, and carried the fight into the American arena. Many evil and stupid men had been sent to the New World as representatives of the crown, but until the Zenger era they were able to keep the press sufficiently in line. It was the misfortune of Colonel William Cosby, one of the worst and stupidest, to collide with a newspaper that would not give way.

In charging Peter Zenger with seditious libel Cosby was acting in accordance with an old habit of the official mind. Until a few years previously, Colonial governors had been specifically commissioned to censor the press, and the tradition still held that journalists had no right to print anything of which the local executive disapproved. His discretion was the criterion, just as the king's was in Britain. He could set down as "libelous" any report that caused him any uneasiness, and impugn it as tending to excite sedition among the governed.

Thus the question of truth was beside the point when printers, publishers, editors, and writers were being prosecuted. Indeed, veracity might only aggravate the charge, for obviously unrest is most likely to follow from a story about stupidity or criminality in government if the news happens to be true. This thought gave rise to a whole theory epitomized in the legal tag, "The greater the truth, the greater the libel." The journalist was caught coming and going—guilty if his story was false, even more guilty if it was true.

Such a theory of seditious libel may sound paradoxical at first, but in fact it had behind it a strong logic based on history. When the British monarchy emerged as absolute during the reign of the Tudors, the relation of king and people was that of master and servants, a relation accepted by the nation almost without demur. Therefore, criticism of the king was illegitimate and *ipso facto* criminal, and the truth of such criticism was at best inconsequential, at worst an exacerbation threatening to cause a breach of the peace. Hence: "The greater the truth, the greater the libel."

But the law could not stop there, for British politics went through a profound revolution during which Parliament wrested control of the government from the king, who slipped steadily downward into the role of servant to, rather than master of, his subjects. Parallel with this development went a progressive rise in the power of the popular will, one result of which was that criticism of king, ministry, and Parliament became transmuted into an integral part of the British system. Now the distinction was no longer between criticism and no criticism, but between valid criticism and invalid criticism; and one acid test was exactly the question of truth in the charges made. By the end of the eighteenth century the change was virtually complete.

The law lagged a little in rewriting its rules. At the time of the Zenger trial (1735) the situation was ambiguous, a fact that comes out clearly in the pleading. Peter Zenger's acquittal helped to resolve the ambiguity along the lines of greater freedom.

Governor Cosby stood for the Tudor principle. He might have coined the phrase, "The greater the truth, the greater the libel," so well did it suit him. His regime would not bear scrutiny, for he riddled it with dubious, unethical, and illegal acts of various kinds—ignoring the rules laid down in his instructions from the Board of Trade in London, interfering with the elections and with the courts, boldly appropriating money and land, insulting the people and the Assembly of the Province—and he did not want such things to be aired, least of all in the columns of a weekly that allowed him no respite as it appeared every Monday with its reports about him and his circle of confederates. He failed in every other attempt to silence the *Journal,* and then brought the printer into a court of law to answer the charge of seditious libel.

So far everything was in order. But as soon as the trial got under way things began to go wrong. Andrew Hamilton had come from Philadelphia to speak for the defense; and he, with all the eloquence for which he was famous, propounded the novel theory (novel for America, at least) that freedom of the press is a basic need of society. He insisted that the people have a right to know what their government is doing. He noted that they should be able to complain when they have a grievance against the government, and that a sure, easy, and speedy method of doing this is for them to make their opinions known in the newspapers. He pointed out the converse, that nothing of this is possible as long as the censor can blue-pencil what he chooses, since the censor is, by definition, the administration's man, and does its bidding.

Above all, he drew a sharp line between truth and falsity in reporting the news. Admitting that no one has a right to lie in print any more than in speech, he successfully inserted into the minds of the jurors the notion that an editor should be allowed to plead the authenticity of a story as his justification for publishing it. He got them to agree that the word "false" should be operative and indispensable in the kind of seditious libel of which Peter Zenger stood accused.

Even Hamilton could not see how titanic an issue was joined. He was primarily interested in the problem at hand—to get his client acquitted—but the fact is that in speaking for his own time he was speaking for all time. He would have been a prophet as well as a philosopher if he had seen fully the parting of the ways at which he stood, with the old censorship extending backward into the past, and the new freedom pointing toward the future. It was merit enough that he saw farther than any other man of his period, and that he stated the argument for the emerging principle better than anyone else.

The full import of his victory in court is not yet exhausted, and very likely never will be. As time passes we understand more exactly just how great a blow it would have been if Governor Cosby had been able to kill the magnificent pioneering experiment in independent journalism that the *Journal* was. We appreciate better than our ancestors the overwhelming significance of the trial of Peter Zenger, that for the first time an American practitioner of unfettered news coverage had won a complete and avowed vindication through the orderly official process of a trial by jury.

Ever since, newsmen have looked back on the Zenger case as the origin of their most primordial right. If that right was not promptly conquered everywhere in the Colonies, Peter Zenger had lit the train for a whole series of delayed reactions. The trial touched off discussions about the meaning of libel, showed that existing definitions were defective rather than axiomatic, compelled the authorities to take more account of public opinion before launching lawsuits against their opponents of politics and journalism, and thereby saved other editors and printers from following the old path that led nowhere except to prison.

James Alexander's *Brief Narrative of the Case and Tryal of John Peter Zenger* was widely reprinted after Zenger himself had turned out the first edition, and the text became a classical precedent to which anyone faced with censorship could point. Americans still point to it when freedom of the press is under discussion.

Present-day newsmen have a more professional reason for being grateful to this Colonial printer. Throughout his imprisonment and trial he maintained a steadfast silence about the identity of the men who wrote the contents of the newspaper that he ran through his press; and he thereby gave an enormous impetus to the thesis that a journalist has a right to keep secret the sources of his information. Other printers before Zenger had refused to divulge the names of their contributors, and some achieved the crown of the semimartyr in consequence, but none had ever been given the unanswerable backing of the courts.

Always the formal conditions of Zenger's acquittal must be borne in mind, for his triumph was not just a personal thing, or the wresting of a momentary privilege from an indolent or interested official. It was a legal precedent.

The Zenger case necessarily reflected on American politics. The acquittal of the Defendant involved the condemnation of the Plaintiff, which meant that Governor Cosby's administration was found guilty of the things with which the *Journal* charged it. One more stumbling block was thrown in the path of tyranny, one more support removed from dishonesty in high places.

Cosby had hand-picked his judge to insure control of the court, but never would this kind of illegality be repeated with the same lighthearted contempt for criticism. Never again would any Colonial governor try quite so recklessly and arrogantly to rig elections or to seize land or to play the politician with his Council in order to create within it a faction that would rubber-stamp his whims. These misdemeanors had been condemned (by implication) in a cold legal decision—and the Colonies would not forget.

The behavior of courts handling libel cases changed. When the New York jury came in with a verdict of "Not guilty," it did something that was rather startling for the 1730's. According to the traditional theory of law, the business of jurors was to determine the fact of publication, and to leave the verdict to the court. In this case, the jury should have confined itself to deciding by whom the *Journal* had been printed and at whom the contents were aimed, after which its function would have been fulfilled. The setup was ideal for Governor Cosby since he had his henchman on the bench, Chief Justice James Delancey, all prepared to render a verdict of "Guilty" as soon as the jury had agreed on the undeniable (and undenied) fact that Peter Zenger was actually printer of the newspaper.

Andrew Hamilton scrambled the neat pattern that Cosby had laid out. He made his appeal directly to the jury, ostentatiously bypassing the judges on the bench, presenting past instances in which jurors had taken upon themselves the responsibility of deciding the law—that is, of giving the verdict, instead of merely identifying the printer of the supposedly libelous material. He argued that juries are of little use if they do not perform this function, since there is no reason for jurors to participate in any trial except that as local citizens they are supposed to be familiar with the facts pertinent to the case. He asked the Zenger jurors simply to declare what they knew to be the truth, that "Zenger's paper" had correctly described the New York administration under which they all lived and suffered. In other words, he appealed to the twelve men in the jury box to take the decision away from a governor-controlled court.

Hamilton got his wish. The jury followed his advice, ignored a warning from Chief Justice Delancey that the verdict was none of their business and should be left to the court, and brought in a finding of "Not guilty." The immediate effect was the acquittal of Peter Zenger. But the long-range effect was a change in the mutual relations of judges and juries. Just as the principle, "The greater the truth, the greater the libel," became more and more implausible as time passed, so did the notion that the proper function of the jury is to determine the "fact," that of judges to hand down the "law." Jurors, like newsmen, were voted a charter of independence at the same time that Peter Zenger was set free.

The Zenger case assisted the rise of public opinion as a factor in American life. The feeling of the inhabitants was never, of course, completely inconsequential, and more than one governor had found himself with a rebellion on his hands when he made himself too obnoxious, but in Peter Zenger's time the people were becoming increasingly restive and impatient under maladministration. He made the attitude vocal as it never had been before. Dissidents had habitually issued critical pamphlets about things they objected to. The *New York Weekly Journal* changed criticism from intermittent to permanent. The newspaper appeared regularly every week, always crammed with information about the officials of New York, and drawing its material from dozens of plain citizens as well as from a steady "staff" of anti-Cosbyites. Because of the *Journal*'s popularity, a whole section of the people received a constant diet of critical journalism that showed them how influential their approval or disapproval was.

Before long popular sentiment constituted a real power in the Colonies. Governors became more reluctant to coerce opposition. Grand juries were emboldened to make freer decisions when called on to indict editors. A witness to the increased importance of the common man is Cadwallader Colden. He became lieutenant-governor of New York, and as such a defender of the crown's prerogative; but he was a veteran of the Zenger controversy, and in the midst of an even greater crisis (that following the Stamp Act) he gave it as his considered opinion that to prosecute newspapermen for libel would be very dangerous in view of the feeling among the people. Journalists became bolder in their criticism, more sure of themselves when they had public opinion with them.

The *New York Weekly Journal* set the classic example of marshaling the citizenry in serried ranks to support one point of view in politics, nor does it, in this, have to take a back seat to any other news organ in the history of American journalism. Sam Adams' *Boston Gazette* but followed in the path already marked out by "Zenger's paper," which was then, and still remains, a model of the art of diverting popular sympathy from individuals and parties by making them look ridiculous or criminal or both.

The participation of ordinary men and women in political discussions, debates, and quarrels caused a rise toward the level of true democracy. The *Journal* proved the close connection between political freedom and freedom of the press half a century before Jefferson laid down his famous axiom on the subject, and a century before de Tocqueville perceived that modern democracy cannot exist without the public forum of the newspapers. By creating political journalism in the true sense, the *Journal* did as much, perhaps, as any other single agent to create the American way of life. If we find censorship stifling today, we owe that phenomenon of our moral physiology in no small degree to the battle that was fought and won by Peter Zenger.

On the constitutional side, the Zenger case helped snap the leading strings that bound the American Colonies to the mother country.

It made resistance to governors more respectable. Governor Cosby's defeat, like Peter Zenger's vindication, was a legal precedent. At no time was there any question of violence or armed insurrection (although Cosby affected to believe the contrary in his letters to London). The thing was fought out strictly through the judicial machinery of the Province, with each side struggling to win over judges and juries. Cosby lost because he could not control the one jury at the critical moment. The decision was unassailable in any legitimate fashion, and Cosby was *ipso facto* legitimately discredited.

The outcome touched off reactions throughout the other Colonies. The published account of the trial was hailed as a notable addition to the documentation of freedom—something to be referred to whenever the liberties of the subject were endangered. No longer could anyone claim with any kind of justice that resistance to crown officials was always wrong, that it had no real basis in American legal development or political experience: the *Brief Narrative of the Case and Tryal of John Peter Zenger* was always there to give the lie to the proposition. When resistance became really outspoken in the time of Adams and Otis and Hancock, its leaders could thank Peter Zenger as one of their forerunners who helped generate the mental atmosphere in which revolutionary ideas could grow, thrive, and spread.

Resistance to governors led directly to resistance to the crown. Until the time of the Zenger case, it had been conventional to solve American problems by British experience, to look to the common tradition for both principles and their correct application. After 1735 that procedure was no longer to be accepted without quibble. Speaking to the jury, Andrew Hamilton based his argument on the common sense notion that British law, as such, could not always apply to America, because conditions in the New World were in many respects unique, that in such cases our law would have to develop its own rules and regulations.

Hamilton referred only to legal development since he was defending a client in a court of law; but from his premise a political conclusion could be drawn, namely, that government might not necessarily be directly transferable either: if the Hanoverian monarchy, however successful in Britain, could not rule satisfactorily the Colonial democracy that was developing on this side of the Atlantic, then perhaps something else should be put in its place. In Hamilton's time the crown itself was not yet suspect; it remained inviolate, the *sanctum sanctorum* of allegiance and veneration, when its representatives over here were attacked with unmitigated animosity. Hamilton himself remarked that the king differed from his officials in kind rather than merely in degree.

Once, however, the authority of the king had been challenged, then Hamilton's appeal from British precedent to Colonial experience became very much to the point. His efforts in behalf of liberty for New York helped pave the way for liberty for America, the rebels of the 1770's drawing from his legal premise the political conclusion that lay implicit in it. He enabled them to argue cogently that independence was not a scandalous novelty but a natural issue of the American situation in the face of an authority three thousand miles away.

The men of the Revolution were well aware of their indebtedness. Gouverneur Morris spoke for them all when he delivered his famous judgment that "The trial of Zenger in 1735 was the morning star of that liberty which subsequently revolutionized America."

Britain herself did not go unaffected by what had happened in the City Hall of her New York Colony. As far as it concerned freedom of the press, the Zenger case fell into place in a transition that had long been developing in the classical home of libertarian ideas. The account of the trial was reprinted there, and cited as an ideal of what British journalists were striving for. In 1738 a London correspondent wrote to Benjamin Franklin's *Pennsylvania Gazette* to say that Andrew Hamilton's address to the jury was causing something of a furor in the coffeehouses where the gentry and the intelligentsia met, as well as among the professional lawyers. The correspondent quoted one leader of the British bar as saying of Hamilton's argument, "If it is not law, it is better than law, it ought to be law, and will always be law wherever justice prevails."

The two great principles—that truth may be used as a defense in libel cases, and that the jury has a right to decide on both the "fact" and the "law"—did eventually become legal for both Britain and America. The process of formal acceptance took time, and the mother country divided with her former Colonies the primacy of writing them into the lawbooks. Britain gave the jury its proper function as early as 1792, with the Fox Libel Act, whereas America had to wait for the Sedition Act of 1798; but we admitted that veracity might be alleged in the Sedition Act, a right which the British were without until Lord Campbell's Act was passed in 1843.

The struggle for the two principles on both sides of the Atlantic is a monument to the sagacity of Andrew Hamilton. No one could have won their vindication at a single stroke against the inertia of old tradition and habitual usage. But he defended them at the critical moment when change had become a real possibility, and did it so powerfully as to give them a forward drive that could not be stopped. Their triumph was therefore his—at the remove of half a century and more.

The current of ideas set in motion by the Zenger case continued throughout the nineteenth century, and became an integral part of journalism as we know it. Libel suits did not diminish; on the contrary, they increased; but they did not follow the lines of the Zenger prosecution. They were mainly suits against "false, scandalous, and malicious" statements in the newspapers, the growing number of such cases reflecting the widening latitude within which editors worked. The word "false" retained the significance that Andrew Hamilton had attributed to it back in 1735. If the threat of the libel action still hung over the heads of journalists (as it rightly did and does), it was not the "libel" that Chief Justice James Delancey had tried to pin on Peter Zenger.

The name of the Colonial printer did not, however, gleam as brightly as it should have in the age of Bennett and Greeley and Raymond and Dana. He was, if not forgotten, at least overlooked or ignored to a surprising extent. Naturally he found a place in the volumes on his art—in Isaiah Thomas' *History of Printing in America*, a masterpiece that appeared in 1810, and in Charles Hildeburn's *Sketches of Printers and Printing in Colonial New York* at the other end of the century (1895). The astonishing thing is that no major work on the Zenger case was written for more than a hundred and fifty years after it.

The twentieth century redressed the balance with Livingston Rutherfurd's *John Peter Zenger, His Press, His Trial and a Bibliography of Zenger Imprints* (1904), which, with all its defects, remains the only attempt to treat Peter Zenger and his newspaper extensively and completely. With its full reprint of the trial, it is the standard work on the subject. The past fifty years have produced a mass of periodical essays, learned monographs, and printed documents on the Zenger case; and, of course, we can interpret the event more intelligently through our added experience of how the press fares under tyrannies so abominable that they leave Governor Cosby looking like a rather mild specimen of the juvenile delinquent.

The memory of Peter Zenger was given a fillip in 1933, the year of the bicentennial of the founding of the *New York Weekly Journal*. In October a distinguished group of newsmen gathered at St. Paul's Church in Eastchester to commemorate the first issue of "Zenger's paper"—that being the place where the Popular party won the election (in spite of Cosby's attempt to rig it) that was the feature story on November 5, 1733. The New York Public Library participated in the celebrations of 1933 by giving an exhibition of its Zenger material. In January of 1934 Senator Borah read into the *Congressional Record* the words from a tablet which the New York Bar Association set up to the memory of Andrew Hamilton: the inscription mentions how Hamilton came from Philadelphia to defend Peter Zenger:

and thus early in the history of the colony of New York, in connection with the events out of which the accusation arose, contributed to the foundation and the subsequent establishment in the American Colonies and the United States of America of the now cherished principles of constitutional liberty, freedom of the press, independence of the judiciary, independence of the bar, freedom of elections and independence of the jury.

These words Senator Borah considered of such moment to the American people and their government that they ought to be permanently enshrined in the proceedings of the national legislature—and so they are.

Fittingly enough, New York City paid the final tribute to one of her great sons. In 1953 was established the John Peter Zenger Memorial Room. Located in the old Sub-Treasury Building, which stands on the site of the City Hall in which Zenger was first imprisoned and then tried, the Memorial Room depicts various scenes from the life and career of the German immigrant who looms so large in the history of our journalism and of our free institutions.

This tribute does not take Peter Zenger out of living history to place him in a museum. Rather does it emphasize the truth that his memory will never die as long as American democracy survives. Interest in his trial should never flag if only because freedom of the press is not something that can be taken for granted. In our time the Communist and Fascist challenges have compelled us to go back to our national origins to justify our way of life. That way of life stands or falls with the right of journalists to criticize the government. We cannot afford to ignore or slur over the printer and his colleagues who first insisted on independence in publishing the news, put their principle into practice, produced a great newspaper that magnificently vindicated them, defended their newspaper in the teeth of official condemnation and judicial indictment, and were so obviously in the right that a jury of their fellow citizens upheld them in spite of a hostile court. Peter Zenger was never more of a portent and a precedent than he is today.

3. The Text

This edition of the trial is, like all others, based on *A Brief Narrative of the Case and Tryal of John Peter Zenger, Printer of the New York Weekly Journal*, which was edited by James Alexander and printed by the Zenger press in 1736.

Alexander's is the only authentic version, for he was the sole person close to the affair who undertook to prepare a written text. He was in this, as in so many other ways, the formal apologist for his side. A rival edition would have been logical, and could easily have been produced by the men of the prosecution, but they never saw fit to attempt their own vindication.

Indeed, Attorney General Bradley declined even to participate in publication, withholding his notes and his brief when the Zenger camp asked to see them, refusing any kind of advice, comment, correction, or even objection; obviously because, staggered and humiliated by the acquittal, he was in no mood to help embalm his courtroom defeat in print. It is a pity that he allowed his case to go by default. He could not, of course, have changed the pleading as we find it set down, except possibly for minor points of emphasis or phraseology, but he might have made a more respectable showing than he does in the bare synopses to which the *Brief Narrative* is reduced from time to time. True, he might have appeared in an even worse light; perhaps he was afraid that that was exactly what his opponents had in mind. Nevertheless, at the very least he would have allowed the public and posterity to view what happened from his angle of vision. He deliberately chose not to do so.

The defense had no inhibitions about publishing a full account of the trial. The cheering and shouting had scarcely died away before Alexander was at work copying out the arguments, arranging notes, gathering information from those who could fill in the gaps for him.

He was the obvious man for the job. Writer, journalist, and editor, he had been schooled in the task of integrating written material and in working up connecting links and explanatory passages as they were needed. Again, not only did he stand near the head of the legal profession, so that he was fully equipped to juggle the problem of libel, the textbook citations, and the technicalities and philosophy of the law (essentials in dealing with any such trial), but he had an unparalleled position at the center of the Zenger turmoil.

No one in New York knew more than James Alexander about how and why Peter Zenger came to be tried before the Supreme Court of the Colony. How could it have been otherwise when the *New York Weekly Journal* was under fire, and Alexander was the *Journal's* editor? He himself had approved, and perhaps written, the "libelous" issues on which the prosecution was based. He himself would have been in the dock as defendant instead of the printer if only the attorney general had been able to get him indicted.

Alexander had been a leader of the Popular party from the beginning of its struggle with Governor Cosby. He had conspired against the Governor, fought him in the Courts and through the press, and used every weapon to hand in an all-out effort to ruin him politically. There was hardly a dissident movement in New York with which Alexander was not allied as adviser or mentor. It was only natural that he should have been one of Zenger's lawyers, for he understood as few others could just what the administration attack amounted to, and how a counterattack should be developed. It is not difficult to imagine the intelligence and the alertness with which he noted every word that was spoken at the trial. He must have been the perfect spectator if ever there was one.

And all this does not exhaust the depths of his familiarity with the incident. Until his disbarment he had been one of the counsel for the defense, which made it his duty to draw up a brief in preparation for his plea. He fulfilled his duty so well that when he was summarily removed by order of Chief Justice Delancey he was able to hand over to Andrew Hamilton a whole plan of campaign, and Hamilton (brought in unprepared and at the last moment) relied on it substantially throughout the proceedings.

It takes nothing from Hamilton, whose performance remains one of the classical things in the history of American law, that Alexander gave him the lead which he followed with such stunning success—that is, the decision to base Zenger's defense on the truth of the *Journal* articles, and on that basis to ask the jury to bring in a verdict of "Not guilty." Alexander already held that guiding thread in his hand months before Hamilton appeared on the scene. (Not that he invented the idea, but he saw that it was the gambit to play.)

Hamilton's own record of the trial went into the *Brief Narrative*, as is indicated by this passage from one of the letters that the Philadelphia barrister wrote to his friend and colleague in New York:

I have at last sent you my draft of Mr. Zenger's trial.... I have had no time to read it over but once since it was finished. I wrote it by half-sheets and copied it as fast as I wrote. The meaning of all this is to beg you to alter and correct it agreeable to your own mind.[36]

Thus Alexander even edited the text submitted by the defense attorney, and the latter's acceptance of the result shows how faithfully it reflected the spoken word. Alexander clearly has given us the events of August 4, 1735, almost to the life.

His account had an enormous success in his own time. Lawyers, journalists, and political philosophers felt the impact of the acquittal as something new, either hopeful or foreboding, and there sprang up a market for the text in both America and England. Other editions began to appear to meet the demand, several of them published in London as early as 1738. The eighteenth century, when the problems involved were still fighting issues, was the golden age of Zenger republication. One of these versions, that issued by J. Almon of London in 1765, is generally available today in the form of a reprint prepared by the Work Projects Administration and sponsored by the California State Library for its series of "Occasional Papers" (1940).

The nineteenth century saw two particularly useful editions in T. B. Howell's *State Trials* (1816) and in Peleg W. Chandler's *American Criminal Trials* (1841), the first following Alexander almost word for word, the second modified and abridged. With the turn of the century Livingston Rutherfurd made available a literal reprint of the *Brief Narrative* in his *John Peter Zenger, His Press, His Trial and a Bibliography of Zenger Imprints* (1904). Fifty years later Frank Luther Mott did the same for our generation in *Oldtime Comments on Journalism* (1954).

The first edition of any text (putting aside the corrupt or otherwise unreliable) always has a presumption in its favor. This is how the author saw his own work; this is the form in which he cast his own thoughts; this is the union of his own logic with his own rhetoric. Nothing else can begin to approach the authority and authenticity of his imprimatur. Consequently it is mandatory for later editors to justify tampering with the text instead of simply reproducing it.

The justification for the version here presented of James Alexander's *A Brief Narrative of the Case and Tryal of John Peter Zenger, Printer of the New York Weekly Journal* is that his text of 1736, however fine an achievement for his own time, is not quite so satisfactory after the lapse of two hundred years. Literary conventions have changed too much for so characteristic a piece of eighteenth-century writing to be allowed to remain as it is when modern standards of readability are in question. Moreover, in places it shows signs of haste, or possibly even of another writer at work. An instance is the opening passage, which falls far below Alexander's best style, and may be by someone else, perhaps Zenger himself. Lastly, there is too much technical law for the lay reader. On all these counts the *Brief Narrative* needs overhauling for our purposes.

This does not imply any distortion: the bulk of Alexander's text is here just as it came from Zenger's press. Most of the pamphlet is still perfectly clear, and it would be pointless to change anything simply for the sake of change. More than that, it is preferable to keep to the original wherever possible in order to catch something of the eighteenth-century atmosphere.

Clarity is the touchstone. Nothing has been allowed to stand that might trouble readers who are not familiar with obsolete usages. The simplest revision is in the spelling, where I use "trial" instead of "tryal," "jail" instead of "gaol," "public" instead of "publick," etc. More important is the change in punctuation. Like most publications of its time, the *Brief Narrative* shows a plethora of commas, colons, and semicolons, a type of punctuation that tends to produce long, complicated, tedious sentences. There are too many capitals and italics, which today not only irritate the eye but also lose their force by doing too much duty. In certain places the grammar calls for the addition or omission of words.

A comparison of the following passages, the first two from the original, the second pair from my edition of the text, will show exactly what changes these considerations have led to:

As There was but one Printer in the Province of *New-York*, that printed a publick News Paper, I was in Hopes, if I undertook to publish another, I might make it worth my while; and I soon found my Hopes were not groundless: My first Paper was printed, *Nov. 5th*, 1733. and I continued printing and publishing of them, I thought to the Satisfaction of every Body, till the *January* following: when the Chief Justice was pleased to animadvert upon the Doctrine of Libels, in a long Charge given in that Term to the

Grand Jury, and afterwards on the third *Tuesday* of *October*, 1734. was again pleased to charge the Grand Jury in the following Words. "*Gentlemen*; I shall conclude...."

Be it remembered, that *Richard Bradly*, Esq: Attorney General of Our Sovereign Lord the King, for the Province of *New-York*, who for Our said Lord the King in this Part prosecutes, in his own proper Person comes here into the Court of our said Lord the King, and for our said Lord the King gives the Court here to understand and be informed, That *John Peter Zenger*, late of the City of *New-York*, Printer, (being a seditious Person; and a frequent Printer and Publisher of false News and seditious Libels, and wickedly and maliciously devising the Government of Our said Lord the King of this His Majesty's Province of *New-York*, under the Administration of His Excellency *William Cosby*, Esq; Captain General and Governour, in Chief of the said Province, to traduce, scandalize and vilify, and His Excellency the said Governour, and the Ministers and Officers of Our said Lord, the King of and for the said Province to bring into Suspicion and the ill Opinion of the Subjects of Our said Lord the King residing within the Province) the Twenty eighth Day of *January*, in the seventh Year of the Reign of Our Sovereign Lord *George* the second, by the Grace of God of *Great-Britain, France* and *Ireland*, King Defender of the Faith, &c. at the City of *New-York*, *did falsly, seditiously and scandalously* print and publish, and cause to be printed and published, a certain *false, malicious, seditious scandalous* Libel, entitled *The New-York Weekly Journal, containing the freshest Advices, foreign and domestick*;

In the present edition, these passages read as follows:

As there was but one printer in the Province of New York who printed a public newspaper, I was in hopes that if I undertook to publish another I might make it worth my while. I soon found my hopes were not groundless. My first paper was printed on November 5, 1733; and I continued printing and publishing them, I thought to the satisfaction of everybody, till the January following, when the Chief Justice was pleased to animadvert upon the doctrine of libels in a long "charge" given in that term to the grand jury. Afterwards, on the third Tuesday of October, 1734, he was again pleased to charge the grand jury in the following words: "Gentlemen, I shall conclude...."

Be it remembered that Richard Bradley, Attorney General of the king for the Province of New York, who prosecutes for the king in this part, in his own proper person comes here into the Court of the king, and for the king gives the Court here to understand and be informed:

That John Peter Zenger, of the City of New York, printer (being a seditious person; and a frequent printer and publisher of false news and seditious libels, both wickedly and maliciously devising the administration of His Excellency

William Cosby, Captain General and Governor in Chief, to traduce, scandalize and vilify both His Excellency the Governor and the ministers and officers of the king, and to bring them into suspicion and the ill opinion of the subjects of the king residing within the Province), on the twenty-eighth day of January, in the seventh year of the reign of George the Second, at the City of New York did falsely, seditiously and scandalously print and publish, and cause to be printed and published, a certain false, malicious, seditious, scandalous libel entitled *The New York Weekly Journal*.

> The major departure from Alexander's text remains to be mentioned, since it is not involved in these passages—namely, the excision of some parts and the summarizing of others. Summaries are used when a faster pace seems advisable, for example at the start, when the preliminary maneuverings of the Governor are described. The excisions concern mainly the technicalities of the law. The long quotations from dusty legal tomes, the appeal to long-past precedents, can be of little interest to any except those trained in the law, and so only those passages have been retained that are necessary to the intelligibility of the arguments. But that in itself means a solid core, enough to show the dialectic of the lawyers moved, how the prosecution set up positions, and how the defense knocked them over.

> Four fifths of the *Brief Narrative* are here—including all the passages-at-arms between Andrew Hamilton on the one side, and Bradley and Delancey on the other, and all of the defense attorney's splendid peroration on liberty that clinched the acquittal for Peter Zenger.

NOTE: Editorial summaries are enclosed within brackets. Other changes are not indicated, and anyone interested in them should consult the original. In particular, blank lines do not necessarily stand for the deletion of material: they are there mainly for convenience in following the case step by step.

Part Two.
The Trial

1. Dramatis Personae

JAMES ALEXANDER, a lawyer for the Defendant

RICHARD BRADLEY, Attorney General

JOHN CHAMBERS, Counsel for the Defense

JAMES DELANCEY, Chief Justice of the Supreme Court

ANDREW HAMILTON, Counsel for the Defense

FRANCIS HARISON, Recorder for the City of New York

FREDERICK PHILIPSE, Associate Justice of the Supreme Court

WILLIAM SMITH, a lawyer for the Defendant

JOHN PETER ZENGER, the Defendant

2. Preliminaries

As there was but one printer in the Province of New York who printed a public newspaper, I[2] was in hopes that if I undertook to publish another I might make it worth my while. I soon found my hopes were not groundless. My first paper was printed on November 5, 1733; and I continued printing and publishing them, I thought to the satisfaction of everybody, till the January following, when the Chief Justice was pleased to animadvert upon the doctrine of libels in a long "charge" given in that term to the grand jury. Afterwards, on the third Tuesday of October, 1734, he was again pleased to charge the grand jury in the following words:

"Gentlemen, I shall conclude with reading a paragraph or two out of the same book concerning libels. They are arrived to that height that they call loudly for your animadversion. It is high time to put a stop to them. For at the rate things are now carried on, when all order and government is endeavored to be trampled on, and reflections are cast upon persons of all degrees, must not these things end in sedition, if not timely prevented? Lenity you have seen will not avail. It becomes you then to inquire after the offenders, that we may in a due course of law be enabled to punish them. If you, gentlemen, do not interpose, consider whether the ill consequences that may arise from any disturbances of the public peace may not in part lie at your door?

"Hawkins,[1] in his chapter on libels, considers, first what shall be said to be a libel, and secondly who are liable to be punished for it. Under the first he says:

Nor can there be any doubt but that a writing which defames a private person only is as much a libel as that which defames persons intrusted in a public capacity, inasmuch as it manifestly tends to create ill blood, and to cause a disturbance of the public peace. However, it is certain that it is a very high aggravation of a libel that it tends to scandalize the government, by reflecting on those who are intrusted with the administration of public affairs; which does not only endanger the public peace, as all other libels do, by stirring up the parties immediately concerned in it to acts of revenge, but also has a direct tendency to breed in the people a dislike of their governors, and incline them to faction and sedition.

"As to the second point, he says:

It is certain that not only he who composes or procures another to compose it but also that he who publishes, or procures another to publish it, are in danger of being punished for it. And it is not material whether he who dispersed a libel knew anything of the contents or effects of it or not; for nothing could be more easy than to publish the most virulent papers with the greatest security if concealing the purport of them from an illiterate publisher would make him safe in dispersing them.

"These, gentlemen, are some of the offenses which are to make part of your inquiries. If any other should arise in the course of your proceedings, in which you are at a loss or conceive any doubts, upon your application here we will assist and direct you."

The grand jury not indicting me as was expected, the gentlemen of the Council proceeded to take my *Journals* into consideration, and sent the following message to the Assembly:

[*The message asked the Assembly to appoint a committee to act with one from the Council. The committees met and decided that the wishes of the Council should be reduced to writing, which was done in these terms*]:

"Gentlemen, the matters we request your concurrence in are that Zenger's papers, Nos. 7, 47, 48, 49—which were read, and which we now deliver—be burned by the hands of the common hangman, as containing in them many things derogatory of the dignity of His Majesty's government, reflecting upon the legislature and upon the most considerable persons in the most distinguished stations in the Province, and tending to raise seditions and tumults among the people thereof.

"That you concur with us in addressing the Governor to issue his proclamation with a promise of reward for the discovery of the authors or writers of these seditious libels.

"That you concur with us in an order for prosecuting the printer thereof.

"That you concur with us in an order to the magistrates to exert themselves in the execution of their offices in order to preserve the public peace of the Province."

[*The Assembly flatly refused its concurrence, and the letter from the Council was returned to it along with the copies of the* Journal *that were marked for burning.*]

On Tuesday, November 5, 1734, the Quarter Sessions for the City of New York began, when the sheriff delivered to the Court an order which was read in these words:

"*Whereas* by an order of this Council some of John Peter Zenger's journals, entitled *The New York Weekly Journal*, Nos. 7, 47, 48, 49, were ordered to be burned by the hands of the common hangman or whipper near the pillory in this city on Wednesday the 6th between the hours of 11 and 12 in the forenoon, as containing in them many things tending to sedition and faction, to bring His Majesty's government into contempt, and to disturb the peace thereof, and containing in them likewise not only reflections upon His Excellency the Governor in particular, and the legislature in general, but also upon the most considerable persons in the most distinguished stations in this Province;

"*It is therefore ordered* that the mayor and magistrates of this city do attend at the burning of the several papers or journals aforesaid, numbered as above mentioned."

Upon reading of which order, the Court forbade the entering thereof in their books at that time, and many of them declared that if it should be entered they would have their protest entered against it.

On Wednesday, November 6, the sheriff of New York moved the Court of Quarter Sessions to comply with the said order, upon which one of the aldermen offered a protest which was read by the clerk and approved by all the aldermen, either expressly or by not objecting to it, and is as follows:

"*Whereas* an order has been served on this Court;

"And *whereas* this Court conceives that they are only to be commanded by the king's mandatory writs, authorized by law, to which they conceive that they have the right of showing cause why they do not obey them if they believe them improper to be obeyed; or by orders which have some known laws to authorize them;

"And *whereas* this Court conceives this order to be no mandatory writ warranted by law, nor knows of no law that authorizes making the order aforesaid, so they think themselves under no obligation to obey it. Which obedience they think would be in them the opening of a door for arbitrary commands, which, when once opened, they know not what dangerous consequences may attend it;

"*Therefore* this Court conceives itself bound in duty (for the preservation of the rights of this Corporation, and, as much as they can, of the liberty of the press and of the people of the Province, since the Assembly of the Province and several grand juries have refused to meddle with the papers when applied to by the Council) to protest against the order aforesaid, and to forbid all the members of this Corporation to pay any obedience to it until it be shown to this Court that the same is authorized by some known law, which they neither know nor believe that it is."

Upon the reading of which it was required of the honorable Francis Harison, recorder of this Corporation and one of the members of the Council (who was present at the making of the said order), to show by what law or authority the said order was made. Upon which he spoke in support of it, and cited the case of Doctor Sacheverell's sermon,[2] which was by the House of Lords ordered to be burned by the hands of the hangman, and that the mayor and aldermen of London should attend the doing of it.

To which one of the aldermen answered to this purpose, that he conceived the case was no ways parallel because Doctor Sacheverell and his sermon were impeached by the House of Commons of England, which is the grand jury of the nation and representative of the whole people of England. That this, their impeachment, they prosecuted before the House of Lords, the greatest court of justice of Britain, and which beyond the memory of man has had cognizance of things of that nature. That Sacheverell had a fair hearing in defense of himself and his sermon. And after that fair hearing he and his sermon were justly, fairly, and legally condemned. That he had read the case of Doctor Sacheverell, and thought he could charge his memory that the judgment of the House of Lords in that case was that only the mayor and sheriffs of London and Middlesex should attend the burning of the sermon, and not the aldermen; and further he remembered that the order upon that judgment was only directed to the sheriffs of London, and not even to the mayor, who did not attend the doing of it. And farther said that would Mr. Recorder show that the Governor and Council had such authority as the House of Lords, and that the papers ordered to be burned were in like manner legally prosecuted and condemned, there the case of Doctor Sacheverell might be to the purpose. But without showing that, it rather proved that a censure ought not to be pronounced till a fair trial by a competent and legal authority were first had.

Mr. Recorder was desired to produce the books from whence he cited his authorities, that the court might judge of them themselves; and was told that if he could produce sufficient authorities to warrant this order they would readily obey it, but not otherwise. Upon which he said that he did not carry his books around with him. To which it was answered that he might send for them, or order a constable to fetch them. Upon which he arose, and at the lower end of the table he mentioned that Bishop Burnet's pastoral letter was ordered by the House of Lords to be burned by the high bailiff of Westminster.[3] Upon which he abruptly went away without waiting for an answer or promising to bring his books, and did not return.

After Mr. Recorder's departure it was moved that the protest should be entered. To which it was answered that the protest could not be entered without entering also the order, and that it was not fit to take any notice of it; and therefore it was proposed that no notice should be taken in their books of either, which was unanimously agreed to by the court.

The sheriff then moved that the court would direct their whipper to perform the said order. To which it was answered that as he was an official of the Corporation they would give no such order. Soon after the court adjourned, and did not attend the burning of the papers.

Afterwards, about noon, the sheriff, after reading the numbers of the several papers which were ordered to be burned, delivered them into the hands of his own Negro and ordered him to put them into the fire, which he did. Mr. Recorder and several of the officers of the garrison attended.

On the Lord's Day, November 17, 1734, I was taken and imprisoned by virtue of a warrant in these words:

"At a Council held at Fort George in New York, November 2, 1734. Present: His Excellency William Cosby, Captain General and Governor in Chief, Mr. Clarke, Mr. Harison, Mr. Livingston, Mr. Kennedy, the Chief Justice, Mr. Cortlandt, Mr. Lane, Mr. Horsmanden.

"It is ordered that the sheriff for the City of New York do forthwith take and apprehend John Peter Zenger for printing and publishing several seditious libels dispersed throughout his journals or newspapers, entitled *The New York Weekly Journal*, as having in them many things tending to raise factions and tumults among the people of this Province, inflaming their minds with contempt of His Majesty's government, and greatly disturbing the peace thereof. And upon his taking the said John Peter Zenger, to commit him to the prison or common jail of the said city and county."

And being by virtue of that warrant so imprisoned in the jail, I was for several days denied the use of pen, ink and paper, and the liberty of speech with any persons.

[*Zenger's lawyers, James Alexander and William Smith, got a habeas corpus, and then argued before the court that their client had a right to reasonable bail. In support of their case they appealed to English law and precedent.*]

Sundry other authorities and arguments were produced and insisted on by my counsel to prove my right to be admitted to moderate bail, and to such bail as was in my power to give. Sundry parts of history they produced to show how much the requiring of excessive bail had been resented by Parliament. And in order to enable the court to judge what surety was in my power to give, I made affidavit that (my debts paid) I was not worth forty pounds (the tools of my trade and wearing apparel excepted).

Some warm expressions (to say no worse of them) were dropped on this occasion, sufficiently known and resented by the listeners, which for my part I desire may be buried in oblivion. In the end it was ordered that I might be admitted to bail, myself in 400 pounds with two sureties, each in 200 pounds, and that I should be remanded till I gave it.

As this was ten times more than was in my power to countersecure any person in giving bail for me, I conceived that I could not ask any to become my bail on these terms; and therefore I returned to the jail, where I lay until Tuesday, January 28, 1735, the last day of the court term. Then, the grand jury having found nothing against me, I expected to be discharged from my imprisonment. But my hopes proved vain, for the attorney general then charged me by "information" for printing and publishing parts of my *Journals* Nos. 13 and 23 as being "false, scandalous, malicious and seditious."

[*When the Court reconvened, Alexander and Smith impugned the right of the Chief Justice, James Delancey, and his colleague, Frederick Philipse, to preside over the case. The lawyers took the position that the commissions of Delancey and Philipse were defective because, among other things, Governor Cosby had appointed the two judges without the consent of his Council, and "at pleasure" instead of "during good behavior."*]

Mr. Alexander offered the above "exceptions" to the Court and prayed that they might be filed. Upon this the Chief Justice said to Mr. Alexander and Mr. Smith that they ought well to consider the consequences of what they offered. To which both answered that they had well considered what they offered, and all the consequences. Mr. Smith added that he was so well satisfied of the right of the subject to take an exception to the commission of a judge, if he thought such commission illegal, that he durst venture his life upon that point. As to the validity of the exceptions then offered, he said he took that to be a second point, but was ready to argue them both, if Their Honors were pleased to hear him. To which the Chief Justice replied that he would consider the exceptions in the morning, and ordered the clerk to bring them to him.

On Wednesday, April 16, 1735, the Chief Justice delivered one of the exceptions to the clerk, and to Justice Philipse the other, upon which Mr. Smith arose and asked the judges whether Their Honors would hear him.

To which the Chief Justice said that they would neither hear nor allow the exceptions. "For," said he, "you thought to have gained a great deal of applause and popularity by opposing this Court; but you have brought it to that point that either we must go from the bench or you from the bar. Therefore we exclude you and Mr. Alexander from the bar." He delivered a paper to the clerk and ordered it to be entered, which the clerk entered accordingly, and returned the paper to the Chief Justice. After which the Chief Justice ordered the clerk to read publicly what he had written, an attested copy whereof follows:

"James Alexander and William Smith, attorneys of this Court, having presumed (notwithstanding they were forewarned by the Court of their displeasure if they should do it) to sign, and having actually signed and put into Court, exceptions in the name of John Peter Zenger, thereby denying the legality of the judges' commissions (though in the usual form) and the being of this Supreme Court;

"*It is therefore ordered* that, for the said contempt, the said James Alexander and William Smith be excluded from any farther practice in this Court, and that their names be struck out of the roll of attorneys of this Court."

After the order of the Court was read, Mr. Alexander asked whether it was the order of Mr. Justice Philipse as well as of the Chief Justice? To which both answered that it was their order.

Mr. Alexander added that it was proper to ask the question that they might know how to have their relief. He further observed to the Court, upon reading of the order, that they were mistaken in their wording of it because the exceptions were only to their commissions, and not to the being of the Court, as is therein alleged; and prayed that the order might be altered accordingly. The Chief Justice said they conceived the exceptions were against the being of the Court. Both Mr. Alexander and Mr. Smith denied that they were, and prayed the Chief Justice to point to the place that contained such exception. They further added that the Court might well exist although the commissions of all the judges were void; which the Chief Justice confessed to be true. Therefore they prayed again that the order in that point might be altered. But it was denied.

[At a meeting of the Court two days later Alexander and Smith asked for a ruling on the extent to which they were affected by the Court order.]

They both also mentioned that it was a doubt whether by the words of the order they were debarred of their practice as counsel as well as attorneys, whereas they practiced in both capacities. To which the Chief Justice answered that the order was plain: That James Alexander and William Smith were debarred and excluded from their whole practice at this bar, and that the order was intended to bar their acting both as counsel and as attorneys, and that it could not be construed otherwise. It being asked Mr. Philipse whether he understood the order so, he answered that he did.

Upon this exclusion of my counsel I petitioned the Court to order counsel for my defense, who thereon appointed John Chambers; who pleaded "Not guilty" for me. But as to the point whether my exceptions should be part of the record as was moved by my former counsel, Mr. Chambers thought not proper to speak to it. Mr. Chambers also moved that a certain day in the next term might be appointed for my trial, and for a struck jury. Whereupon my trial was ordered to be on Monday, August 4, and the Court would consider till the first day of next term whether I should have a struck jury or not, and ordered that the sheriff should in the meantime, at my charge, return the Freeholders book.

On Tuesday, July 29, 1735, the Court opened. On the motion of Mr. Chambers for a struck jury, pursuant to the rule of the preceding term, the Court were of the opinion that I was entitled to have a struck jury. That evening at five o'clock some of my friends attended the clerk for striking the jury; when to their surprise the clerk, instead of producing the Freeholders book, to strike the jury from it in their presence as usual, produced a list of 48 persons whom he said he had taken out of the Freeholders book.

My friends told him that a great number of these persons were not freeholders; that others were persons holding commissions and offices at the Governor's pleasure; that others were of the late displaced magistrates of this city, who must be supposed to have resentment against me for what I had printed concerning them; that others were the Governor's baker, tailor, shoemaker, candlemaker, joiner, etc.; that as to the few indifferent men that were upon that list, they had reason to believe (as they had heard) that Mr. Attorney had a list of them, to strike them out. And therefore they requested that he would either bring the Freeholders book, and choose out of it 48 unexceptional men in their presence as usual, or else that he would hear their objections particularly to the list he offered, and that he would put impartial men in the place of those against whom they could show just objections.

Notwithstanding this, the clerk refused to strike the jury out of the Freeholders book, and refused to hear any objections to the persons on the list; but told my friends that if they had any objections to any persons, they might strike those persons out. To which they answered that there would not remain a jury if they struck out all the exceptional men, and according to the custom they had a right to strike out only twelve.

Finding no arguments could prevail with the clerk to hear their objections to his list, nor to strike the jury as usual, Mr. Chambers told him that he must apply to the Court; which the next morning he did. And the Court upon his motion ordered that the 48 should be struck out of the Freeholders book as usual, in the presence of the parties, and that the clerk should hear objections to persons proposed to be of the 48, and allow of such exceptions as were just. In pursuance of that order a jury was that evening struck to the satisfaction of both parties. My friends and counsel insisted on no objections but want of freehold, although they did not insist that Mr. Attorney General should show any particular cause against any persons he disliked, but acquiesced that any person he disliked should be left out of the 48.

3. Pleading

Before James Delancey, Chief Justice of the Province of New York, and Frederick Philipse, Associate Justice, my trial began on August 4, 1735, upon an information for printing and publishing two newspapers which were called libels against our Governor and his administration.

The defendant, John Peter Zenger, being called, appeared.

MR. CHAMBERS, *of counsel for the defense.* I humbly move, Your Honors, that we may have justice done by the sheriff, and that he may return the names of the jurors in the same order as they were struck.

MR. CHIEF JUSTICE. How is that? Are they not so returned?

MR. CHAMBERS. No they are not. For some of the names that were last set down in the panel are now placed first.

MR. CHIEF JUSTICE. Make that out and you shall be righted.

MR. CHAMBERS. I have the copy of the panel in my hand as the jurors were struck, and if the clerk will produce the original signed by Mr. Attorney and myself, Your Honor will see that our complaint is just.

MR. CHIEF JUSTICE. Clerk, is it so? Look upon that copy. Is it a true copy of the panel as it was struck?

CLERK. Yes, I believe it is.

MR. CHIEF JUSTICE. How came the names of the jurors to be misplaced in the panel?

SHERIFF. I have returned the jurors in the same order in which the clerk gave them to me.

MR. CHIEF JUSTICE. Let the names of the jurors be ranged in the order they were struck, agreeable to the copy here in Court.

Which was done accordingly; and the jury, whose names were as follows, were called and sworn: Thomas Hunt (Foreman), Harmanus Rutgers, Stanly Holmes, Edward Man, John Bell, Samuel Weaver, Andries Marschalk, Egbert van Borsom, Benjamin Hildreth, Abraham Keteltas, John Goelet, Hercules Wendover.

Mr. Attorney General opened the information, which was as follows:

MR. ATTORNEY. May it please Your Honors and you, Gentlemen of the Jury. The information now before the Court, and to which the defendant, Zenger, has pleaded "Not guilty," is an information for printing and publishing a false, scandalous, and seditious libel in which His Excellency, the Governor of this Province, who is the king's immediate representative here, is greatly and unjustly scandalized as a person that has no regard to law or justice; with much more, as will appear upon reading the information. Libeling has always been discouraged as a thing that tends to create differences among men, ill blood among the people, and oftentimes great bloodshed between the party libeling and the party libeled. There can be no doubt but you, Gentlemen of the Jury, will have the same ill opinion of such practices as judges have always shown upon such occasions. But I shall say no more at this time, until you hear the information, which is as follows:

Be it remembered that Richard Bradley, Attorney General of the king for the Province of New York, who prosecutes for the king in this part, in his own proper person comes here into the Court of the king, and for the king gives the Court her to understand and be informed:

That John Peter Zenger, of the City of New York, printer (being a seditious person; and a frequent printer and publisher of false news and seditious libels, both wickedly and maliciously devising the administration of His Excellency William Cosby, Captain General and Governor in Chief, to traduce, scandalize, and vilify both His Excellency the Governor and the ministers and officers of the king, and to bring them into suspicion and the ill opinion of the subjects of the king residing within the Province), on the twenty-eighth day of January, in the seventh year of the reign of George the Second, at the City of New York did falsely, seditiously, and scandalously print and publish, and cause to be printed and published, a certain false, malicious, seditious, scandalous libel entitled *The New York Weekly Journal*.

In which libel, among other things therein contained, are these words, "Your appearance in print at last gives a pleasure to many, although most wish you had come fairly into the open field, and not appeared behind entrenchments made of the supposed laws against libeling, and of what other men had said and done before. These entrenchments, gentlemen, may soon be shown to you and to all men to be weak, and to have neither law nor reason for their foundation, and so cannot long stand in your stead. Therefore you had much better as yet leave them, and come to what the people of this City and Province (*the City and Province of New York meaning*) think are the points in question. They (*the people of the City and Province of New York meaning*) think, as matters now stand, that their liberties and properties are precarious, and that slavery is like to be entailed on them and their posterity if some past things be not amended, and this they collect from many past proceedings." (*Meaning many of the past proceedings of His Excellency, the Governor, and of the ministers and officers of the king, of and for the said Province.*)

And the Attorney General likewise gives the Court here to understand and be informed:

That the said John Peter Zenger afterwards, to wit on the eighth day of April, did falsely, seditiously and scandalously print and publish another false, malicious, seditious, and scandalous libel entitled *The New York Weekly Journal.*

In which libel, among other things therein contained, are these words, "One of our neighbors (*one of the inhabitants of New Jersey meaning*) being in company and observing the strangers (*some of the inhabitants of New York meaning*) full of complaints, endeavored to persuade them to remove into Jersey. To which it was replied, that would be leaping out of the frying pan into the fire; for, says he, we both are under the same Governor (*His Excellency the said Governor meaning*), and your Assembly have shown with a vengeance what is to be expected from them. One that was then moving to Pennsylvania (*meaning one that was then removing from New York with intent to reside at Pennsylvania*), to which place it is reported that several considerable men are removing (*from New York meaning*), expressed in terms very moving much concern for the circumstances of New York (*the bad circumstances of the Province and people of New York meaning*), and seemed to think them very much owing to the influence that some men (whom he called tools) had in the administration (*meaning the administration of government of the said Province of New York*). He said he was now going from them, and was not to be hurt by any measures they should take, but could not help having some concern for the welfare of his countrymen, and should be glad to hear that the Assembly (*meaning the General Assembly of the Province of New York*) would exert themselves as became them by showing that they have the interest of their country more at heart than the gratification of any private view of any of their members, or being at all affected by the smiles or frowns of a governor (*His Excellency the said Governor meaning*); both of which ought equally to be despised when the interest of their country is at stake.

"You, says he, complain of the lawyers, but I think the law itself is at an end. We (*the people of the Province of New York meaning*) see men's deeds destroyed, judges arbitrarily displaced, new courts erected without consent of the legislature (*within the Province of New York meaning*) by which it seems to me trial by jury is taken away when a governor pleases (*His Excellency the said Governor meaning*), and men of known estates denied their votes contrary to the received practice, the best expositor of any law. Who is there then in that Province (*meaning the Province of New York*) that can call anything his own, or enjoy any liberty, longer than those in the administration (*meaning the administration of government of the said Province of New York*) will condescend to let them do it? For which reason I have left it, as I believe more will."

These words are to the great disturbance of the peace of the said Province of New York, to the great scandal of the king, of His Excellency the Governor, and of all others concerned in the administration of the government of the Province, and against the peace of the king, his crown, and his dignity.

Whereupon the said Attorney General of the king prays the advisement of the Court here, in the premises, and the due process of law against the said John Peter Zenger.

To this information the defendant has pleaded "Not guilty," but we are ready to prove it.

Mr. Chambers has not been pleased to favor me with his notes, so I cannot, for fear of doing him an injustice, pretend to set down his argument. But here Mr. Chambers set forth very clearly the nature of a libel, the great allowances that ought to be made for what men speak or write, that in all libels there must be some particular persons so clearly pointed out that no doubt must remain about who is meant, that he was in hopes Mr. Attorney would fail in his proof as to this point. And therefore desired that he would go on to examine his witnesses.

Then Mr. Hamilton, who at the request of some of my friends was so kind as to come from Philadelphia to assist me at the trial, spoke.

MR. HAMILTON. May it please Your Honor, I am concerned in this cause on the part of Mr. Zenger, the defendant. The information against my client was sent me a few days before I left home, with some instructions to let me know how far I might rely upon the truth of those parts of the papers set forth in the information, and which are said to be libelous.

Although I am perfectly of the opinion with the gentleman who has just now spoken on the same side with me, as to the common course of proceedings—I mean in putting Mr. Attorney upon proving that my client printed and published those papers mentioned in the information—yet I cannot think it proper for me (without doing violence to my own principles) to deny the publication of a complaint, which I think is the right of every freeborn subject to make when the matters so published can be supported with truth.

Therefore I shall save Mr. Attorney the trouble of examining his witnesses to that point. I do (for my client) confess that he both printed and published the two newspapers set forth in the information—and I hope that in so doing he has committed no crime.

MR. ATTORNEY. Then if Your Honor pleases, since Mr. Hamilton has confessed the fact, I think our witnesses may be discharged. We have no further occasion for them.

MR. HAMILTON. If you brought them here only to prove the printing and publishing of these newspapers, we have acknowledged that, and shall abide by it.

Here my journeyman and two sons (with several others subpoenaed by Mr. Attorney to give evidence against me) were discharged, and there was silence in the Court for some time.

MR. CHIEF JUSTICE. Well, Mr. Attorney, will you proceed?

MR. ATTORNEY. Indeed, Sir, as Mr. Hamilton has confessed the printing and publishing of these libels, I think the Jury must find a verdict for the king. For supposing they were true, the law says that they are not the less libelous for that. Nay, indeed the law says their being true is an aggravation of the crime.

MR. HAMILTON. Not so neither, Mr. Attorney. There are two words to that bargain. I hope it is not our bare printing and publishing a paper that will make it a libel. You will have something more to do before you make my client a libeler. For the words themselves must be libelous—that is, *false, scandalous, and seditious*—or else we are not guilty.

As Mr. Attorney has not been pleased to favor us with his argument, which he read, or with the notes of it, we cannot take upon us to set down his words, but only to show the book cases he cited and the general scope of the argument which he drew from those authorities.

He observed upon the excellency as well as the use of government, and the great regard and reverence which had been constantly paid to it, under both the law and the Gospels. That by government we were protected in our lives, religion, and properties; and for these reasons great care had always been taken to prevent everything that might tend to scandalize magistrates and others concerned in the administration of the government, especially the supreme magistrate. And that there were many instances of very severe judgments, and of punishments, inflicted upon such as had attempted to bring the government into contempt by publishing false and scurrilous libels against it, or by speaking evil and scandalous words of men in authority, to the great disturbance of the public peace. And to support this he cited various legal texts.

From these books he insisted that a libel was a malicious defamation of any person, expressed either in printing or writing, signs or pictures, to asperse the reputation of one that is alive, or the memory of one that is dead. If he is a private man, the libeler deserves a severe punishment, but if it is against a magistrate or other public person, it is a greater offense. For this concerns not only the breach of the peace but the scandal of the government. What greater scandal of government can there be than to have corrupt or wicked magistrates appointed by the king to govern his subjects? A greater imputation to the state there cannot be than to suffer such corrupt men to sit in the sacred seat of justice, or to have any meddling in or concerning the administration of justice.

From the same books Mr. Attorney insisted that whether the person defamed is a private man or a magistrate, whether living or dead, whether the libel is true or false, or if the party against whom it is made is of good or evil fame, it is nevertheless a libel. For in a settled state of government the party grieved ought to complain, for every injury done him, in the ordinary course of the law. And as to its publication, the law had taken so great care of men's reputations that if one maliciously repeats it, or sings it in the presence of another, or delivers the libel or a copy of it over to scandalize the party, he is to be punished as a publisher of a libel.

He said it was likewise evident that libeling was an offense against the law of God. Acts 23:5: Then said Paul, "I wist not, brethren, that he was the high priest; for it is written Thou shalt not speak evil of the ruler of thy people." II Peter 2:10: Despise government. Presumptuous are they, selfwilled, they are not afraid to speak evil of dignities.

He then insisted that it was clear, by the laws of God and man, that it was a very great offense to speak evil of, or to revile, those in authority over us. And that Mr. Zenger had offended in a most notorious and gross manner, in scandalizing His Excellency our governor, who is the king's immediate representative and the supreme magistrate of this Province. For can there be anything more scandalous said of a governor than what is published in those papers? Nay, not only the Governor but both the Council and the Assembly are scandalized. For there it is plainly said that "as matters now stand, their liberties and properties are precarious, and that slavery is like to be entailed on them and their posterity." And then again Mr. Zenger says, "The Assembly ought to despise the smiles or frowns of a governor; that he thinks the law is at an end; that we see men's deeds destroyed, judges arbitrarily displaced, new courts erected without consent of the legislature; that it seems that trials by jury are taken away when a governor pleases; and that none can call anything his own longer than those in the administration will condescend to let him do it."

Mr. Attorney added that he did not know what could be said in defense of a man that had so notoriously scandalized the Governor and the principal magistrates and officers of the government by charging them with depriving the people of their rights and liberties, taking away trial by jury, and, in short, putting an end to the law itself. If this was not a libel, he said, he did not know what was one. Such persons as will take those liberties with governors and magistrates he thought ought to suffer for stirring up sedition and discontent among the people.

He concluded by saying that the government had been very much traduced and exposed by Mr. Zenger before he was taken notice of; that at last it was the opinion of the Governor and the Council that he ought not to be suffered to go on to disturb the peace of the government by publishing such libels against the Governor and the chief persons in the government; and therefore they had directed this prosecution to put a stop to this scandalous and wicked practice of libeling and defaming His Majesty's government and disturbing His Majesty's peace.

Mr. Chambers then summed up to the jury, observing with great strength of reason on Mr. Attorney's defect of proof that the papers in the information were false, malicious, or seditious, which it was incumbent on him to prove to the jury, and without which they could not on their oaths say that they were so as charged.

MR. HAMILTON. May it please Your Honor, I agree with Mr. Attorney that government is a sacred thing, but I differ widely from him when he would insinuate that the just complaints of a number of men who suffer under a bad administration is libeling that administration. Had I believed that to be law, I should not have given the Court the trouble of hearing anything that I could say in this cause.

I own that when I read the information I had not the art to find out (without the help of Mr. Attorney's *innuendos*) that the Governor was the person meant in every period of that newspaper. I was inclined to believe that they were written by some who (from an extraordinary zeal for liberty) had misconstrued the conduct of some persons in authority into crimes; and that Mr. Attorney (out of his too great zeal for power) had exhibited this information to correct the indiscretion of my client, and at the same time to show his superiors the great concern he had lest they should be treated with any undue freedom.

But from what Mr. Attorney has just now said, to wit, that this prosecution was directed by the Governor and the Council, and from the extraordinary appearance of people of all conditions, which I observe in Court upon this occasion, I have reason to think that those in the administration have by this prosecution something more in view, and that the people believe they have a good deal more at stake, than I apprehended. Therefore, as it is become my duty to be both plain and particular in this cause, I beg leave to bespeak the patience of the Court.

I was in hopes—as that terrible Court where those dreadful judgments were given, and that law established, which Mr. Attorney has produced for authorities to support this cause, was long ago laid aside as the most dangerous Court to the liberties of the people of England that ever was known in that kingdom—

that Mr. Attorney, knowing this, would not have attempted to set up a star chamber here, nor to make their judgments a precedent to us. For it is well known that what would have been judged treason in those days for a man to speak, has since not only been practiced as lawful, but the contrary doctrine has been held to be law.

In Brewster's case,[4] for printing that subjects might defend their rights and liberties by arms in case the king should go about to destroy them, he was told by the Chief Justice that it was a great mercy he was not proceeded against for his life; for to say the king could be resisted by arms in any case whatsoever was express treason. And yet we see since that time that Doctor Sacheverell was sentenced in the highest court in Great Britain for saying that such a resistance was not lawful. Besides, as times have made very great changes in the laws of England, so in my opinion there is good reason that places should do so too.

Is it not surprising to see a subject, upon receiving a commission from the king to be a governor of a Colony in America, immediately imagining himself to be vested with all the prerogatives belonging to the sacred person of his prince? And, which is yet more astonishing, to see that a people can be so wild as to allow of and acknowledge those prerogatives and exemptions, even to their own destruction? Is it so hard a matter to distinguish between the majesty of our sovereign and the power of a governor of The Plantations? Is not this making very free with our prince, to apply that regard, obedience, and allegiance to a subject, which is due only to our sovereign?

And yet in all the cases which Mr. Attorney has cited to show the duty and obedience we owe to the supreme magistrate, it is the king that is there meant and understood, although Mr. Attorney is pleased to urge them as authorities to prove the heinousness of Mr. Zenger's offense against the Governor of New York. The several Plantations are compared to so many large corporations, and perhaps not improperly. Can anyone give an instance that the head of a corporation ever put in a claim to the sacred rights of majesty? Let us not (while we are pretending to pay a great regard to our prince and his peace) make bold to transfer that allegiance to a subject which we owe to our king only.

What strange doctrine is it to press everything for law here which is so in England? I believe we should not think it a favor, at present at least, to establish this practice. In England so great a regard and reverence is had to the judges that if any man strikes another in Westminster Hall while the judges are sitting, he shall lose his right hand and forfeit his land and goods for so doing. Although the judges here claim all the powers and authorities within this government that a Court of King's Bench has in England, yet I believe Mr. Attorney will scarcely say that such a punishment could be legally inflicted on a man for committing such an offense in the presence of the judges sitting in any court within the Province of New York. The reason is obvious. A quarrel or riot in New York cannot possibly be attended with those dangerous consequences that it might in Westminster Hall; nor (I hope) will it be alleged that any misbehavior to a governor in The Plantations will, or ought to be, judged of or punished as a like undutifulness would be to our sovereign.

From all of which, I hope Mr. Attorney will not think it proper to apply his law cases (to support the cause of his governor) which have only been judged where the king's safety or honor was concerned.

It will not be denied that a freeholder in the Province of New York has as good a right to the sole and separate use of his lands as a freeholder in England, who has a right to bring an action of trespass against his neighbor for suffering his horse or cow to come and feed upon his land or eat his corn, whether enclosed or not. Yet I believe it would be looked upon as a strange attempt for one man here to bring an action against another whose cattle and horses feed upon his grounds that are not enclosed, or indeed for eating and treading down his corn, if that were not enclosed.

Numberless are the instances of this kind that might be given to show that what is good law at one time and in one place is not so at another time and in another place. So that I think the law seems to expect that in these parts of the world men should take care, by a good fence, to preserve their property from the injury of unruly beasts. And perhaps there may be a good reason why men should take the same care to make an honest and upright conduct a fence and security against the injury of unruly tongues.

MR. ATTORNEY. I don't know what the gentleman means by comparing cases of freeholders in England with freeholders here. What has this case to do with actions of trespass or men's fencing their ground? The case before the Court is whether Mr. Zenger is guilty of libeling His Excellency the Governor of New York, and indeed the whole administration of the government. Mr.

Hamilton has confessed the printing and publishing, and I think nothing is plainer than that the words in the information are "scandalous, and tend to sedition, and to disquiet the minds of the people of this Province." If such papers are not libels, I think it may be said that there can be no such thing as a libel.

MR. HAMILTON. May it please Your Honor, I cannot agree with Mr. Attorney. For although I freely acknowledge that there are such things as libels, yet I must insist at the same time that what my client is charged with is not a libel. And I observed just now that Mr. Attorney, in defining a libel, made use of the words "scandalous, seditious, and tend to disquiet the people." But (whether with design or not I will not say) he omitted the word "false."

MR. ATTORNEY. I think that I did not omit the word "false." But it has been said already that it may be a libel notwithstanding that it may be true.

MR. HAMILTON. In this I must still differ with Mr. Attorney. For I depend upon it that we are to be tried upon this information now before the Court and the jury, and to which we have pleaded "Not guilty." By it we are charged with printing and publishing "a certain false, malicious, seditious, and scandalous libel." This word "false" must have some meaning, or else how came it there? I hope Mr. Attorney will not say he put it there by chance, and I am of the opinion that his information would not be good without it.

But to show that it is the principal thing which, in my opinion, makes a libel, suppose that the information had been for printing and publishing a certain *true* libel, would that be the same thing? Or could Mr. Attorney support such an information by any precedent in the English law? No, the falsehood makes the scandal, and both make the libel. And to show the Court that I am in good earnest, and to save the Court's time and Mr. Attorney's trouble, I will agree that if he can prove the facts charged upon us to be *false*, I shall own them to be *scandalous, seditious, and a libel*. So the work seems now to be pretty much shortened, and Mr. Attorney has now only to prove the words *false* in order to make us guilty.

MR. ATTORNEY. We have nothing to prove. You have confessed the printing and publishing. But if it were necessary (as I insist it is not), how can we prove a negative? I hope some regard will be had to the authorities that have been produced, and that supposing all the words to be true, yet that will not help them. Chief Justice Holt,[5] in his charge to the jury in the case of Tutchin,[6] made no distinction whether Tutchin's papers were true or false; and as Chief Justice Holt has made no distinction in that case, so none ought to be made here; nor can it be shown that, in all that case, there was any question made about their being false or true.

MR. HAMILTON. I did expect to hear that a negative cannot be proved. But everybody knows there are many exceptions to that general rule. For if a man is charged with killing another, or stealing his neighbor's horse, if he is innocent in the one case he may prove the man said to be killed to be really alive, and the horse said to be stolen never to have been out of his master's stable, etc. And this, I think, is proving a negative.

But we will save Mr. Attorney the trouble of proving a negative, take the *onus probandi* on ourselves, and prove those very papers that are called libels to be *true*.

MR. CHIEF JUSTICE. You cannot be admitted, Mr. Hamilton, to give the truth of a libel in evidence. A libel is not to be justified; for it is nevertheless a libel that it is *true*.

MR. HAMILTON. I am sorry the Court has so soon resolved upon that piece of law. I expected first to have been heard to that point. I have not, in all my reading, met with an authority that says we cannot be admitted to give the truth in evidence upon an information for libel.

MR. CHIEF JUSTICE. The law is clear that you cannot justify a libel.

MR. HAMILTON. I own that, may it please Your Honor, to be so. But, with submission, I understand the word "justify" there to be a justification by plea, as it is in the case upon an indictment for murder or an assault and battery. There the prisoner cannot justify, but pleads "Not guilty." Yet it will not be denied but he may be, and always is, admitted to give the truth of the fact, or any other matter, in evidence, which goes to his acquittal. As in murder he may prove that it was in defense of his life, his house, etc.; and in assault and battery he may give in evidence that the other party struck first; and in both cases he will be acquitted. In this sense I understand the word "justify" when applied to the case before the Court.

MR. CHIEF JUSTICE. I pray, show that you can give the truth of a libel in evidence.

[*Here there was a discussion of the point, and Hamilton produced precedents from English law to prove that in the past men accused of libel had been allowed to defend themselves on the ground of the truth of what they wrote.*]

MR. HAMILTON. How shall it be known whether the words are libelous, that is, *true* or *false*, but by admitting us to prove them *true*, since Mr. Attorney will not undertake to prove them *false*? Besides, is it not against common sense that a man should be punished in the same degree for a true libel (if any such thing could be) as for a false one? I know it is said that truth makes a libel the more provoking, and therefore the offense is greater, and consequently the judgment should be the heavier. Well, suppose it were so, and let us agree for once that *truth is a greater sin than falsehood.* Yet, as the offenses are not equal, and as the punishment is arbitrary, that is, according as the judges in their discretion shall direct to be inflicted, is it not absolutely necessary that they should know whether the libel is true or false, that they may by that means be able to proportion the punishment?

For would it not be a sad case if the judges, for want of a due information, should chance to give as severe a judgment against a man for writing or publishing a lie, as for writing or publishing a truth? And yet this, with submission, as monstrous and ridiculous as it may seem to be, is the natural consequence of Mr. Attorney's doctrine that *truth makes a worse libel than falsehood*, and must follow from his not proving our papers to be *false*, or not suffering us to prove them to be *true*.

In the case of Tutchin, which seems to be Mr. Attorney's chief authority, that case is against him; for Tutchin was, at his trial, put upon showing the truth of his papers; but he did not. At least the prisoner was asked by the king's counsel whether he would say that they were *true*. And as he never pretended that they were true, the Chief Justice was not to say so.

But the point will be clearer on our side from Fuller's case.[7] Here you see is a scandalous and infamous charge against the late king; here is a charge no less than high treason, against the men in public trust, for receiving money of the French king, then in actual war with the crown of Great Britain; and yet the Court were far from bearing him down with that star chamber doctrine, to wit, that it was no matter whether what he said was true or false. No, on the contrary, Lord Chief Justice Holt asks Fuller, "Can you make it appear that they are true? Have you any witnesses? You might have had subpoenas for your witnesses against this day. If you take it upon you to write such things as you are charged with, it lies upon you to prove them true, at your peril. If you have any witnesses, I will hear them. How came you to write those books which are not true? If you have any witnesses, produce them. If you can offer any matter to prove what you wrote, let us hear it." Thus said, and thus did, that great man, Lord Chief Justice Holt, upon a trial of the like kind with ours; and the rule laid down by him in this case is *that he who will take upon him to write things, it lies upon him to prove them, at his peril.* Now, sir, we have acknowledged the printing and publishing of those papers set forth in the information, and (with the leave of the Court) agreeable to the rule laid down by Chief Justice Holt, we are ready to prove them to be true, at our peril.

MR. CHIEF JUSTICE. Let me see the book.

Here the Court had the case under consideration a considerable time, and everyone was silent.

MR. CHIEF JUSTICE. Mr. Attorney, you have heard what Mr. Hamilton has said, and the cases he has cited, for having his witnesses examined to prove the truth of the several facts contained in the papers set forth in the information. What do you say to it?

MR. ATTORNEY. The law, in my opinion, is very clear. They cannot be admitted to justify a libel, for by the authorities I have already read to the Court it is not the less a libel because it is true. I think I need not trouble the Court over again. The thing seems to be very plain, and I submit it to the Court.

MR. CHIEF JUSTICE. Mr. Hamilton, the Court is of the opinion that you ought not to be permitted to prove the facts in the papers. These are the words of the book, "It is far from being a justification of a libel that the contents thereof are true, or that the person upon whom it is made had a bad reputation, since the greater appearance there is of truth in any malicious invective, so much the more provoking it is."

MR. HAMILTON. These are star chamber cases, and I was in hopes that that practice had been dead with the court.

MR. CHIEF JUSTICE. Mr. Hamilton, the Court have delivered their opinion, and we expect that you will use us with good manners. You are not to be permitted to argue against the opinion of the Court.

MR. HAMILTON. With submission, I have seen the practice in very great courts, and never heard it deemed unmannerly to—

MR. CHIEF JUSTICE. After the Court have declared their opinion, it is not good manners to insist upon a point in which you are overruled.

MR. HAMILTON. I will say no more at this time. The Court, I see, is against us in this point—and that I hope I may be allowed to say.

MR. CHIEF JUSTICE. Use the Court with good manners and you shall be allowed all the liberty you can reasonably desire.

MR. HAMILTON. I thank Your Honor. Then, Gentlemen of the Jury, it is to you that we must now appeal for witnesses to the truth of the facts we have offered, and are denied the liberty to prove. Let it not seem strange that I apply myself to you in this manner. I am warranted by both law and reason.

The law supposes you to be summoned out of the neighborhood where the fact is alleged to be committed; and the reason of your being taken out of the neighborhood is because you are supposed to have the best knowledge of the fact that is to be tried. Were you to find a verdict against my client, you must take it upon you to say that the papers referred to in the information, and which we acknowledge we printed and published, are *false, scandalous, and seditious*.

But of this I can have no apprehension. You are citizens of New York. You are really what the law supposes you to be, honest and lawful men; and according to my brief, the facts which we offer to prove were not committed in a corner. They are notoriously known to be true. Therefore in your justice lies our safety. And as we are denied the liberty of giving evidence to prove the truth of what we have published, I will beg leave to lay it down as a standing rule in such cases that the suppressing of evidence ought always to be taken for the strongest evidence; and I hope it will have that weight with you.

But since we are not admitted to examine our witnesses, I will endeavor to shorten the dispute with Mr. Attorney, and to that end I desire he would favor us with some standard definition of a libel by which it may be certainly known whether a writing be a libel, yes or no.

MR. ATTORNEY. The books, I think, have given a very full definition of libel.

MR. HAMILTON. Ay, Mr. Attorney, but what standard rule have the books laid down by which we can certainly know whether the words or signs are malicious? Whether they are defamatory? Whether they tend to the breach of the peace, and are a sufficient ground to provoke a man, his family, or his friends to acts of revenge: especially the ironical sort of words? What rule have you to know when I write ironically? I think it would be hard when I say, "Such a man is a very worthy honest gentleman, and of fine understanding," that therefore I mean, "He is a knave or a fool."

MR. ATTORNEY. I think the books are very full. It is said in Hawkins just now read, "Such scandal as is expressed in a scoffing and ironical manner makes a writing as properly a libel as that which is expressed in direct terms." I think nothing can be plainer or more full than these words.

MR. HAMILTON. I agree the words are very plain, and I shall not scruple to allow (when we are agreed that the words are false and scandalous, and were spoken in an ironical and scoffing manner) that they are really libelous. But here still occurs the uncertainty which makes the difficulty to know what words are scandalous, and what are not. For you say that they may be scandalous, whether true or false.

Besides, how shall we know whether the words were spoken in a scoffing and ironical manner, or seriously? Or how can you know whether the man did not think as he wrote? For by your rule, if he did, it is no irony, and consequently no libel.

But under favor, Mr. Attorney, I think the same book, and under the same section, will show us the only rule by which all these things are to be known. The words are these, "which kind of writing is as well *understood* to mean only to upbraid the parties with the want of these qualities as if they had directly and expressly done so." Here it is plain that the words are scandalous, scoffing, and ironical only as they are *understood*. I know no rule laid down in the books but this, I mean, as the words are *understood*.

MR. CHIEF JUSTICE. Mr. Hamilton, do you think it so hard to know when words are ironical or spoken in a scoffing manner?

MR. HAMILTON. I own it may be known. But I insist that the only rule by which to know is—as I do or can *understand* them. I have no other rule to go by but as I *understand* them.

MR. CHIEF JUSTICE. That is certain. All words are libelous or not as they are *understood*. Those who are to judge of the words must judge whether they are scandalous, or ironical, or tend to the breach of the peace, or are seditious. There can be no doubt of it.

MR. HAMILTON. I thank Your Honor. I am glad to find the Court of this opinion. Then it follows that these twelve men must *understand* the words in the information to be scandalous—that is to say, false. For I think it is not pretended they are of the *ironical* sort. And when they *understand* the words to be so, they will say that we are guilty of publishing a *false libel*, and not otherwise.

MR. CHIEF JUSTICE. No, Mr. Hamilton, the jury may find that Zenger printed and published those papers, and leave it to the Court to judge whether they are libelous. You know this is very common. It is in the nature of a special verdict, where the jury leave the matter of the law to the court.

MR. HAMILTON. I know, may it please Your Honor, the jury may do so. But I do likewise know that they may do otherwise. I know that they have the right beyond all dispute to determine both the law and the fact; and where they do not doubt of the law, they ought to do so. Leaving it to judgment of the court whether the words are libelous or not in effect renders juries useless (to say no worse) in many cases. But this I shall have occasion to speak to by and by.

Although I own it to be base and unworthy to scandalize any man, yet I think it is even more villainous to scandalize a person of public character. I will go so far into Mr. Attorney's doctrine as to agree that if the faults, mistakes, nay even the vices of such a person be private and personal, and do not affect the peace of the public, or the liberty or property of our neighbor, it is unmanly and unmannerly to expose them either by word or writing. But when a ruler of a people brings his personal failings, but much more his vices, into his administration, and the people find themselves affected by them either in their liberties or properties, that will alter the case mightily; and all the things that are said in favor of rulers and of dignitaries, and upon the side of power, will not be able to stop people's mouths when they feel themselves oppressed. I mean, in a free government.

MR. ATTORNEY. Pray, Mr. Hamilton, have a care what you say, don't go too far. I don't like those liberties.

MR. HAMILTON. Surely, Mr. Attorney, you won't make any applications. All men agree that we are governed by the best of kings, and I cannot see the meaning of Mr. Attorney's caution. My well-known principles, and the sense I have of the blessings we enjoy under His Majesty, make it impossible for me to err, and I hope even to be suspected, in that point of duty to my king.

May it please Your Honor, I was saying that notwithstanding all the duty and reverence claimed by Mr. Attorney to men in authority, they are not exempt from observing the rules of common justice either in their private or public capacities. The laws of our mother country know no exemptions. It is true that men in power are harder to be come at for wrongs they do either to a private person or to the public, especially a governor in The Plantations, where they insist upon an exemption from answering complaints of any kind in their own government. We are indeed told, and it is true, that they are obliged to answer a suit in the king's courts at Westminster for a wrong done to any person here. But do we not know how impracticable this is to most men among us, to leave their families (who depend upon their labor and care for their livelihood) and carry evidence to Britain, and at a great, nay, a far greater expense than almost any of us are able to bear, only to prosecute a governor for an injury done here?

But when the oppression is general, there is no remedy even that way. No, our Constitution has (blessed be God) given us an opportunity, if not to have such wrongs redressed, yet by our prudence and resolution we may in a great measure prevent the committing of such wrongs by making a governor sensible that it is in his interest to be just to those under his care. For such is the sense that men in general (I mean free men) have of common justice, that when they come to know that a chief magistrate abuses the power with which he is trusted for the good of the people, and is attempting to turn that very power against the innocent, whether of high or low degree, I say that mankind in general seldom fail to interpose, and, as far as they can, prevent the destruction of their fellow subjects.

And has it not often been seen (I hope it will always be seen) that when the representatives of a free people are by just representations or remonstrances made sensible of the sufferings of their fellow subjects, by the abuse of power in the hands of a governor, that they have declared (and loudly too) that they were not obliged by any law to support a governor who goes about to destroy a Province or Colony, or their privileges, which by His Majesty he was appointed, and by the law he is bound, to protect and encourage? But I pray that it may be considered—of what use is this mighty privilege if every man that suffers is silent? And if a man must be taken up as a libeler for telling his sufferings to his neighbor?

I know that it may be answered, "Have you not a legislature? Have you not a House of Representatives to whom you may complain?" To this I answer, we have. But what then? Is an Assembly to be troubled with every injury done by a governor? Or are they to hear of nothing but what those in the administration will please to tell them? And what sort of trial must a man have? How is he to be remedied, especially if the case were, as I have known to happen in America in my time, that a governor who has places (I will not say pensions, for I believe they seldom give that to another which they can take to themselves) to bestow can keep the same Assembly (after he has modeled them so as to get a majority of the House in his interest) for near twice seven years together? I pray, what redress is to be expected for an honest man who makes his complaint against a governor to an Assembly who may properly enough be said to be made by the same governor against whom the complaint is made? The thing answers itself.

No, it is natural, it is a privilege, I will go farther, it is a right, which all free men claim, that they are entitled to complain when they are hurt. They have a right publicly to remonstrate against the abuses of power in the strongest terms, to put their neighbors upon their guard against the craft or open violence of men in authority, and to assert with courage the sense they have of the blessings of liberty, the value they put upon it, and their resolution at all hazards to preserve it as one of the greatest blessings heaven can bestow.

When a House of Assembly composed of honest freemen sees the general bent of the people's inclination, that is it which must and will (I am sure it ought to) weigh with a legislature in spite of all the craft, caressing, and cajoling made use of by a governor to divert them from harkening to the voice of their country. As we all very well understand the true reason why gentlemen take so much pains and make such great interest to be appointed governors, so is the design of their appointment not less manifest.

We know His Majesty's gracious intentions toward his subjects. He desires no more than that his people in The Plantations should be kept up to their duty and allegiance to the crown of Great Britain, that peace may be preserved among them, and justice impartially administered; so that we may be governed so as to render us useful to our mother country by encouraging us to make and raise such commodities as may be useful to Great Britain.

But will anyone say that all or any of these good ends are to be effected by a governor's setting his people together by the ears, and by the assistance of one part of the people to plague and plunder the other? The commission that governors bear while they execute the powers given them according to the intent of the royal grantor requires and deserves very great reverence and submission. But when a governor departs from the duty enjoined on him by his sovereign, and acts as if he were less accountable than the royal hand that gave him all that power and honor that he is possessed of, this sets people upon examining and inquiring into the power, authority, and duty of such a magistrate, and to comparing those with his conduct. And just as far as they find he exceeds the bounds of his authority, or falls short in doing impartial justice to the people under his administration, so far they very often, in return, come short in their duty to such a governor.

For power alone will not make a man beloved, and I have heard it observed that the man who was neither good nor wise before his being made a governor never mended upon his preferment, but has been generally observed to be worse. For men who are not indued with wisdom and virtue can only be kept in bounds by the law; and by how much the further they think themselves out of the reach of the law, by so much the more wicked and cruel men are. I wish there were no instances of the kind at this day.

Wherever this happens to be the case of a governor, unhappy are the people under his administration, and in the end he will find himself so too, for the people will neither love him nor support him.

I make no doubt but there are those here who are zealously concerned for the success of this prosecution, and yet I hope they are not many; and even some of those, I am persuaded (when they consider to what lengths such prosecutions may be carried, and how deeply the liberties of the people may be affected by such means) will not all abide by their present sentiments. I say "not all," for the man who from an intimacy and acquaintance with a governor has conceived a personal regard for him, the man who has felt none of the strokes of his power, the man who believes that a governor has a regard for him and confides in him—it is natural for such men to wish well to the affairs of such a governor. And as they may be men of honor and generosity, may, and no doubt will, wish him success so far as the rights and privileges of their fellow citizens are not affected. But as men of honor I can apprehend nothing from them. They will never exceed that point.

There are others that are under stronger obligations, and those are such as are in some sort engaged in support of the governor's cause by their own or their relations' dependence on his favor for some post or preferment. Such men have what is commonly called duty and gratitude to influence their inclinations and oblige them to go his lengths. I know men's interests are very near to them, and they will do much rather than forgo the favor of a governor and a livelihood at the same time. But I can with very just grounds hope, even from those men (whom I will suppose to be men of honor and conscience too), that when they see the liberty of their country in danger, either by their concurrence or even by their silence, they will like Englishmen, and like themselves, freely make a sacrifice of any preferment or favor rather than be accessory to destroying the liberties of their country and entailing slavery upon their posterity.

There are indeed another set of men, of whom I have no hopes. I mean such who lay aside all other considerations and are ready to join with power in any shape, and with any man or sort of men by whose means or interest they may be assisted to gratify their malice and envy against those whom they have been pleased to hate; and that for no other reason than because they are men of ability and integrity, or at least are possessed of some valuable qualities far superior to their own. But as envy is the sin of the Devil, and therefore very hard (if at all) to be repented of, I will believe there are but few of this detestable and worthless sort of men, nor will their opinions or inclinations have any influence upon this trial.

But to proceed. I beg leave to insist that the right of complaining or remonstrating is natural; that the restraint upon this natural right is the law only; and that those restraints can only extend to what is *false*. For as it is truth alone that can excuse or justify any man for complaining of a bad administration, I as frankly agree that nothing ought to excuse a man who raises a false charge or accusation even against a private person, and that no manner of allowance ought to be made to him who does so against a public magistrate.

Truth ought to govern the whole affair of libels. And yet the party accused runs risk enough even then; for if he fails in proving every tittle of what he has written, and to the satisfaction of the court and jury too, he may find to his cost that when the prosecution is set on foot by men in power it seldom wants friends to favor it.

From thence (it is said) has arisen the great diversity of opinions among judges about what words were or were not scandalous or libelous. I believe it will be granted that there is not greater uncertainty in any part of the law than about words of scandal. It would be misspending of the Court's time to mention the cases. They may be said to be numberless. Therefore the utmost care ought to be taken in following precedents; and the times when the judgments were given, which are quoted for authorities in the case of libels, are much to be regarded.

I think it will be agreed that ever since the time of the Star Chamber, where the most arbitrary judgments and opinions were given that ever an Englishman heard of, at least in his own country; I say, prosecutions for libel since the time of that arbitrary Court, and until the Glorious Revolution, have generally been set on foot at the instance of the crown or its ministers. And it is no small reproach to the law that these prosecutions were too often and too much countenanced by the judges, who held their places "at pleasure" (a disagreeable tenure to any officer, but a dangerous one in the case of a judge). Yet I cannot think it unwarrantable to show the unhappy influence that a sovereign has sometimes had, not only upon judges, but even upon parliaments themselves.

It has already been shown how the judges differed in their opinions about the nature of a libel in the case of the Seven Bishops.[8] There you see three judges of one opinion, that is, of a wrong opinion (in the judgment of the best men in England), and one judge of a right opinion. How unhappy might it have been for all of us at this day if that jury had understood the words in that information as the Court did? Or if they had left it to the Court to judge whether the petition of the Bishops was or was not a libel? No, they took upon them (to their immortal honor!) to determine both *law* and *fact*, and to *understand* the petition of the Bishops to be *no libel*, that is, to contain no falsehood or sedition; and therefore found them not guilty.

If then upon the whole there is so great an uncertainty among judges (learned and great men) in matters of this kind, if power has had so great an influence on judges, how cautious ought we to be in determining by their judgments, especially in The Plantations, and in the case of libels?

There is heresy in law as well as in religion, and both have changed very much. We well know that it is not two centuries ago that a man would have been burned as a heretic for owning such opinions in matters of religion as are publicly written and printed at this day. They were fallible men, it seems, and we take the liberty not only to differ from them in religious opinions, but to condemn them and their opinions too. I must presume that in taking these freedoms in thinking and speaking about matters of faith or religion, we are in the right; for although it is said that there are very great liberties of this kind taken in New York, yet I have heard of no information preferred by Mr. Attorney for any offenses of this sort. From which I think it is pretty clear that in New York a man may make very free with his God, but he must take a special care what he says of his governor.

It is agreed upon by all men that this is a reign of liberty. While men keep within the bounds of truth I hope they may with safety both speak and write their sentiments of the conduct of men in power—I mean of that part of their conduct only which affects the liberty or property of the people under their administration. Were this to be denied, then the next step may make them slaves; for what notions can be entertained of slavery beyond that of suffering the greatest injuries and oppressions without the liberty of complaining, or if they do, to be destroyed, body and estate, for so doing?

It is said and insisted on by Mr. Attorney that government is a sacred thing; that it is to be supported and reverenced; that it is government that protects our persons and estates, prevents treasons, murders, robberies, riots, and all the train of evils that overturns kingdoms and states and ruins particular persons. And if those in the administration, especially the supreme magistrate, must have all their conduct censured by private men, government cannot subsist. This is called a licentiousness not to be tolerated. It is said that it brings the rulers of the people into contempt, and their authority not to be regarded, and so in the end the laws cannot be put into execution.

These, I say, and such as these, are the general topics insisted upon by men in power and their advocates. But I wish it might be considered at the same time how often it has happened that the abuse of power has been the primary cause of these evils, and that it was the injustice and oppression of these great men that has commonly brought them into contempt with the people. The craft and art of such men is great, and who that is the least acquainted with history or law can be ignorant of the specious pretences that have often been made use of by men in power to introduce arbitrary rule, and to destroy the liberties of a free people?

[*Here Hamilton went back to legal history to strengthen his position on the right of a defendant to plead truth in libel cases, and on the right of the jury to determine both the law and the fact—that is, to deliver a verdict of guilty or not guilty of libel, instead of leaving that culminating decision to the judges on the bench.*]

This is the second information for libeling of a governor that I have known in America. The first, although it may look like a romance, yet as it is true I will beg leave to mention it.

Governor Nicholson,[9] who happened to be offended with one of his clergy, met him one day upon the road; and as usual with him (under the protection of his commission) used the poor parson with the worst of language, and threatened to cut off his ears, slit his nose, and at last to shoot him through the head. The parson, being a reverend man, continued all this time uncovered in the heat of the sun, until he found an opportunity to fly for it. Coming to a neighbor's house, he felt himself very ill of a fever, and immediately writes for a doctor. And that his physician might the better judge of his distemper, he acquainted him with the usage he had received; concluding that the Governor was certainly mad, for that no man in his senses would have behaved in that manner.

The doctor unhappily showed the parson's letter. The Governor came to hear of it. And so an information was preferred against the poor man for saying he believed the Governor was mad. It was laid down in the information to be false, scandalous, and wicked, and written with intent to move sedition among the people, and to bring His Excellency into contempt. But by an order from the late Queen Anne there was a stop put to that prosecution, with sundry others set on foot by the same Governor against gentlemen of the greatest worth and honor in that government.

And may not I be allowed, after all this, to say that by a little countenance almost anything that a man writes may, with the help of that useful term of art called an *innuendo*, be construed to be a libel, according to Mr. Attorney's definition of it—to wit, that whether the words are spoken of a person of a public character or of a private man, whether dead or living, good or bad, true or false, all make a libel. For according to Mr. Attorney, after a man hears a writing read, or reads and repeats it, or laughs at it, they are all punishable. It is true that Mr. Attorney is so good as to allow it must be after the party knows it to be a libel, but he is not so kind as to take the man's word for it.

Here were several cases put to show that although what a man writes of a governor were true, proper, and necessary, yet according to the foregoing doctrine it might be construed to be a libel. But Mr. Hamilton, after the trial was over, being informed that some of the cases he had put had really happened in this government, declared that he had never heard of any such; and as he meant no personal reflections, he was sorry he had mentioned them, and therefore they are omitted here.

MR. HAMILTON. If a libel is understood in the large and unlimited sense urged by Mr. Attorney, there is scarce a writing I know that may not be called a libel, or scarce a person safe from being called to an account as a libeler. For Moses, meek as he was, libeled Cain; and who is it that has not libeled the Devil?

For according to Mr. Attorney it is no justification to say that one has a bad name. Echard has libeled our good King William;[10] Burnet has libeled, among others, King Charles and King James; and Rapin has libeled them all.[11] How must a man speak or write; or what must he hear, read, or sing; or when must he laugh so as to be secure from being taken up as a libeler?

I sincerely believe that were some persons to go through the streets of New York nowadays and read a part of the Bible, if it was not known to be such, Mr. Attorney (with the help of his *innuendos*) would easily turn it into a libel. As for instance Isaiah 9:16: "The leaders of the people cause them to err; and they that are led by them are destroyed." Should Mr. Attorney go about to make this a libel, he would read it thus: The leaders of the people (*innuendo, the Governor and Council of New York*) cause them (*innuendo, the people of this Province*) to err, and they (*the people of this Province meaning*) that are led by them (*the Governor and Council meaning*) are destroyed (*innuendo, are deceived into the loss of their liberty*), which is the worst kind of destruction.

Or if some person should publicly repeat, in a manner not pleasing to his betters, the 10th and 11th verses of the 56th chapter of the same book, there Mr. Attorney would have a large field to display his skill in the artful application of his *innuendos*. The words are: "His watchmen are blind, they are all ignorant,... Yea, they are greedy dogs which can never have enough." To make them a libel there is, according to Mr. Attorney's doctrine, no more wanting but the aid of his skill in the right adapting of his *innuendos*. As for instance: His watchmen (*innuendo, the Governor's Council and his Assembly*) are blind, they are all ignorant (*innuendo, will not see the dangerous designs of His Excellency*). Yea, they (*the Governor and Council meaning*) are greedy dogs which can never have enough (*innuendo, enough of riches and power*).

Such an instance as this seems only fit to be laughed at; but I appeal to Mr. Attorney himself whether these are not at least equally proper to be applied to His Excellency and his ministers as some of the inferences and *innuendos* in his information against my client. Then if Mr. Attorney is at liberty to come into court and file an information in the king's name, without leave, who is secure whom he is pleased to prosecute as a libeler?

And give me leave to say that the mode of prosecuting by information (when a grand jury will not find a true bill) is a national grievance, and greatly inconsistent with that freedom that the subjects of England enjoy in most other cases. But if we are so unhappy as not to be able to ward off this stroke of power directly, yet let us take care not to be cheated out of our liberties by forms and appearances. Let us always be sure that the charge in the information is made out clearly even beyond a doubt; for although matters in the information may be called *form* upon trial, yet they may be, and often have been found to be, matters of *substance* upon giving judgment.

Gentlemen: The danger is great in proportion to the mischief that may happen through our too great credulity. A proper confidence in a court is commendable, but as the verdict (whatever it is) will be yours, you ought to refer no part of your duty to the discretion of other persons. If you should be of the opinion that there is no falsehood in Mr. Zenger's papers, you will, nay (pardon me for the expression) you ought, to say so—because you do not know whether others (I mean the Court) may be of that opinion. It is your right to do so, and there is much depending upon your resolution as well as upon your integrity.

The loss of liberty, to a generous mind, is worse than death. And yet we know that there have been those in all ages who, for the sake of preferment, or some imaginary honor, have freely lent a helping hand to oppress, nay to destroy, their country.

This brings to my mind that saying of the immortal Brutus[12] when he looked upon the creatures of Caesar, who were very great men but by no means good men. "You Romans," said Brutus, "if yet I may call you so, consider what you are doing. Remember that you are assisting Caesar to forge those very chains that one day he will make you yourselves wear." This is what every man (who values freedom) ought to consider. He should act by judgment and not by affection or self-interest; for where those prevail, no ties of either country or kindred are regarded; as upon the other hand, the man who loves his country prefers its liberty to all other considerations, well knowing that without liberty life is a misery.

A famous instance of this you will find in the history of another brave Roman of the same name, I mean Lucius Junius Brutus,[13] whose story is well known, and therefore I shall mention no more of it than only to show the value he put upon the freedom of his country. After this great man, with his fellow citizens whom he had engaged in the cause, had banished Tarquin the Proud (the last king of Rome) from a throne that he ascended by inhuman murders and possessed by the most dreadful tyranny and proscriptions, and had by this means amassed incredible riches, even sufficient to bribe to his interest many of the young nobility of Rome to assist him in recovering the crown; the plot being discovered, the principal conspirators were apprehended, among whom were two of the sons of Junius Brutus. It was absolutely necessary that some should be made examples of, to deter others from attempting the restoration of Tarquin and destroying the liberty of Rome. To effect this it was that Lucius Junius Brutus, one of the consuls of Rome, in the presence of the Roman people, sat judge and condemned his own sons as traitors to their country. And to give the last proof of his exalted virtue and his love of liberty, he with a firmness of mind (only becoming so great a man) caused their heads to be struck off in his own presence. When he observed that his rigid virtue occasioned a sort of horror among the people, it is observed that he said only, "My fellow citizens, do not think that this proceeds from any want of natural affection.

No, the death of the sons of Brutus can affect Brutus only. But the loss of liberty will affect my country."

Thus highly was liberty esteemed in those days, that a father could sacrifice his sons to save his country. But why do I go to heathen Rome to bring instances of the love of liberty? The best blood in Britain has been shed in the cause of liberty; and the freedom we enjoy at this day may be said to be (in a great measure) owing to the glorious stand the famous Hampden,[14] and others of our countrymen, made against the arbitrary demands and illegal impositions of the times in which they lived; who, rather than give up the rights of Englishmen and submit to pay an illegal tax of no more, I think, than three shillings, resolved to undergo, and for the liberty of their country did undergo, the greatest extremities in that arbitrary and terrible Court of the Star Chamber, to whose arbitrary proceedings (it being composed of the principal men of the realm, and calculated to support arbitrary government) no bounds or limits could be set, nor could any other hand remove the evil but Parliament.

Power may justly be compared to a great river. While kept within its due bounds it is both beautiful and useful. But when it overflows its banks, it is then too impetuous to be stemmed; it bears down all before it, and brings destruction and desolation wherever it comes. If, then, this is the nature of power, let us at least do our duty, and like wise men (who value freedom) use our utmost care to support liberty, the only bulwark against lawless power, which in all ages has sacrificed to its wild lust and boundless ambition the blood of the best men that ever lived.

I hope to be pardoned, Sir, for my zeal upon this occasion. It is an old and wise caution that when our neighbor's house is on fire we ought to take care of our own. For though (blessed be God) I live in a government where liberty is well understood and freely enjoyed, yet experience has shown us all (I am sure it has to me) that a bad precedent in one government is soon set up for an authority in another. And therefore I cannot but think it my, and every honest man's, duty that (while we pay all due obedience to men in authority) we ought at the same time to be upon our guard against power wherever we apprehend that it may affect ourselves or our fellow subjects.

I am truly very unequal to such an undertaking on many accounts. You see that I labor under the weight of many years, and am bowed down with great infirmities of body. Yet, old and weak as

I am, I should think it my duty, if required, to go to the utmost part of the land where my services could be of any use in assisting to quench the flame of prosecutions upon informations, set on foot by the government to deprive a people of the right of remonstrating (and complaining too) of the arbitrary attempts of men in power.

Men who injure and oppress the people under their administration provoke them to cry out and complain, and then make that very complaint the foundation for new oppressions and prosecutions. I wish I could say that there were no instances of this kind.

But to conclude. The question before the Court and you, Gentlemen of the Jury, is not of small or private concern. It is not the cause of one poor printer, nor of New York alone, which you are now trying. No! It may in its consequence affect every free man that lives under a British government on the main of America. It is the best cause. It is the cause of liberty. And I make no doubt but your upright conduct this day will not only entitle you to the love and esteem of your fellow citizens, but every man who prefers freedom to a life of slavery will bless and honor you as men who have baffled the attempt of tyranny, and by an impartial and uncorrupt verdict have laid a noble foundation for securing to ourselves, our posterity, and our neighbors, that to which nature and the laws of our country have given us a right— the liberty of both exposing and opposing arbitrary power (in these parts of the world at least) by speaking and writing truth.

Here Mr. Attorney observed that Mr. Hamilton had gone very much out of the way, and had made himself and the people very merry; but that he had been citing cases not at all to the purpose. All that the jury had to consider was Mr. Zenger's printing and publishing two scandalous libels that very highly reflected on His Excellency and the principal men concerned in the administration of this government—which is confessed. That is, the printing and publishing of the journals set forth in the information is confessed. He concluded that as Mr. Hamilton had confessed the printing, and there could be no doubt but they were scandalous papers highly reflecting upon His Excellency and on the principal magistrates in the Province—therefore he made no doubt but that the jury would find the defendant guilty, and would refer to the Court for their directions.

MR. CHIEF JUSTICE. Gentlemen of the Jury: The great pains Mr. Hamilton has taken to show how little regard juries are to pay to the opinion of judges, and his insisting so much upon the conduct of some judges in trials of this kind, is done no doubt with a design that you should take but very little notice of what I might say upon this occasion. I shall therefore only observe to you that as the facts or words in the information are confessed, the only thing that can come in question before you is whether the words as set forth in the information make a libel. And that is a matter of law, no doubt, and which you may leave to the Court.

MR. HAMILTON. I humbly beg Your Honor's pardon, I am very much misapprehended if you suppose that what I said was so designed.

Sir, you know I made an apology for the freedom that I found myself under a necessity of using upon this occasion. I said there was nothing personal designed. It arose from the nature of our defense.

The jury withdrew, and returned in a small time. Being asked by the clerk whether they were agreed on their verdict, and whether John Peter Zenger was guilty of printing and publishing the libels in the information mentioned, they answered by Thomas Hunt, their foreman, "Not guilty." Upon which there were three huzzas in the hall, which was crowded with people; and the next day I was discharged from my imprisonment.

4. Aftermath

At a Common Council held at the City Hall on Tuesday, September 16, 1735:

"*Ordered*, that Andrew Hamilton of Philadelphia, barrister-at-law, be presented with the Freedom of this Corporation."

At a Common Council held at the City Hall on Monday, September 29, 1735: Paul Richards (Mayor), the Recorder, aldermen, and assistants of the City of New York, convened in Common Council.

"To all to whom these presents shall come, greeting.

"*Whereas* honor is the just reward of virtue, and public benefits demand a public acknowledgment;

"*We therefore*, under a grateful sense of the remarkable service done to the inhabitants of this City and Colony by Andrew Hamilton of Pennsylvania, barrister-at-law—by his learned and generous defense of the rights of mankind and the liberty of the press in the case of John Peter Zenger, lately tried on an information exhibited in the Supreme Court of this Colony—do by these presents bear to the said Andrew Hamilton the public thanks of the Freemen of this Corporation for that signal service which he cheerfully undertook under great indisposition of body and generously performed, refusing any fee or reward;

"And in testimony of our great esteem for his person, and sense of his merit, do hereby present him with the Freedom of this Corporation.

"These are therefore to certify and declare that the said Andrew Hamilton is hereby admitted, received, and allowed a Freeman of the said City; to have, hold, enjoy, and partake of all the benefits, liberties, privileges, freedoms, and immunities whatsoever granted or belonging to a Freeman and Citizen of the same City.

"In testimony whereof, the Common Council of the City, in Common Council assembled, have caused the Seal of the City to be hereunto affixed this twenty-ninth day of September, Anno Domini one thousand seven hundred and thirty-five."

Appendix I

The New York Weekly Journal Covers an Election

The Westchester election in which Lewis Morris won his most satisfying victory over Governor Cosby took place on the green of St. Paul's Church, Eastchester, on October 29, 1733. Whoever wrote the *Journal's* story about the election was no mean hand at covering the news, as the following extracts will show:

> On this day Lewis Morris, late Chief Justice of this Province, was by a great majority of voices elected a Representative for the County of Westchester.

> This being an election of great expectation, and wherein the court and country's interest was exerted (as is said) to the utmost, I shall give my readers a particular account of it as I had it from a person that was present at it.

> Nicholas Cooper, high sheriff of the said county, having by papers affixed to the church of Eastchester and other public places given notice of the day and place of election, without mentioning any time of the day when it was to be done, made the electors on the side of the late judge very suspicious that some fraud was intended; to prevent which about fifty of them kept watch upon and about the green at Eastchester (the place of election) from 12 o'clock the night before until the morning of that day.

> The other electors beginning to move on Sunday afternoon and evening so as to be at New Rochelle by midnight, their way lay through Harrison's Purchase, the inhabitants of which provided for their entertainment as they passed, each house in their way having a table plentifully covered for that purpose. About midnight they all met at the house of William Lecount in New Rochelle, whose house not being large enough to entertain so great a number, a large fire was made in the street, by which they sat until daylight, at which time they began to move. They were joined on the hill at the east end of the town by about seventy horse of the electors of the lower part of the county, and then proceeded towards the place of election in the following order.

> First rode two trumpeters and three violins; next four of the principal freeholders, one of whom carried a banner on one side of which was affixed in gold capitals KING GEORGE, and on the other, in like golden capitals, LIBERTY AND LAW; next followed the candidate, Lewis Morris, late Chief Justice of this

Province; then two colors; and at sunrise they entered upon the green of Eastchester, the place of the election, followed by about three hundred horse of the principal freeholders of the county (a greater number than had ever appeared for one man since the settlement of that county).

About eleven of the clock appeared the candidate of the other side, William Forster, schoolmaster, appointed by the Society for Propagation of the Gospel, and lately made by commission from His Excellency (the present Governor) Clerk of the Peace and Common Pleas in that county; which commission it is said he purchased for the valuable consideration of one hundred pistoles given the Governor. Next to him came two ensigns borne by two of the freeholders; then followed the Honorable James Delancey, Chief Justice of the Province of New York, and the Honorable Frederick Philipse, second judge of the said Province and Baron of the Exchequer, attended by about one hundred seventy horse of the freeholders and friends of the said Forster. The two judges entered the green on the east side, and as they rode twice around it their greeting was "No land tax!" as they passed. The second judge very civilly saluted the late Chief Justice by taking off his hat, which the late judge returned in the same manner.

About an hour after the high sheriff came to town finely mounted, the housings and holster caps being scarlet richly laced with silver.... Upon his approach the electors on both sides went into the green where they were to elect; and after having read His Majesty's writ he bade the electors to proceed to the choice, which they did. A great majority appeared for Mr. Morris, upon which a poll was demanded, but by whom is not known to the relator, though it was said by many to be done by the sheriff himself. Morris, the candidate, several times asked the sheriff upon whose side the majority appeared, but could get no other reply but that a poll must be had.

Accordingly, after about two hours' delay in getting benches, chairs, and tables, they began to poll. Soon after one of those called Quakers, a man of known worth and estate, came to give his vote for the late judge. Upon this Forster and the two Fowlers, Moses and William, chosen by him to be inspectors, questioned his having an estate, and required of the sheriff to tender him the Book to swear in due form of law; which he refused to do, but offered to take his solemn affirmation, which by both the laws of England and the laws of this Province was indulged to the people called Quakers, and had always been practiced from the first election of Representatives in this Province to this time, and never refused. But the sheriff was deaf to all that could be alleged on that side; and notwithstanding that he was told by both the late Chief Justice and James Alexander, one of His Majesty's Council and counsellor-at-law, and by William Smith, counsellor-at-law, that such a procedure was contrary to law and a violent attempt on the liberties of the people, he still persisted in refusing the said Quaker to vote; and in like manner did refuse seven and thirty Quakers more, men of known and visible estates. About eleven o'clock that night the poll was closed, and it stood thus:

For the late Chief Justice	231
Quakers	38
In all	269
For William Forster	151
The difference	118
	269

So that the late Chief Justice carried it by a great majority without the Quakers.

The indentures being sealed, the whole body of electors waited on their new Representative to his lodgings with trumpets sounding and violins playing; and in a little time took their leave of him. Thus ended the Westchester election, to the general satisfaction.

New York, November 5.

On Wednesday the 31st of October the late Chief Justice, but new Representative for the County of Westchester, landed in this city about five o'clock in the evening at the ferry stairs. On his landing he was saluted by a general fire of the guns from the merchant vessels lying in the road; and was received by great numbers of the most considerable merchants and inhabitants of this city, and by them, with loud acclamations of the people as he walked the streets, conducted to the Black Horse Tavern, where a handsome entertainment was prepared for him at the charge of the gentlemen who received him. In the middle of one side of the room was fixed a tabulet with golden capitals, *KING GEORGE, LIBERTY AND LAW.*

Appendix II

Zenger's Lawyers on the Behavior of His Judges

James Alexander and William Smith, disbarred for their exceptions to the commissions of the two Justices of the Supreme Court, won reinstatement in their practice after an appeal to the legislature. Their appeal was printed by Peter Zenger under the title, *The Complaint of James Alexander and William Smith to the Committee of the General Assembly of the Colony of New York* (1735). Here is the centerpiece of their argument:

> We conceived the innocence of our client no sufficient security while we esteemed the Governor his prosecutor, who had the judges in his power. We had too much reason for caution from the conduct of the Chief Justice. We heard how His Honor had vented his displeasure against him when he accidentally met him in the street on the Sunday before his arrest. We had been witnesses to sundry warm charges and moving addresses to several grand juries plainly leveled against Zenger, and with intention to procure his country to indict him. And we saw his name among that committee of the Council that conferred with a committee of this House in order to procure a concurrence to condemn some of Zenger's *Journals* without giving him an opportunity to defend them. We heard that the Chief Justice was a principal manager at that conference and spoke much on that occasion. We saw his name among those who issued that order of the Council that commanded the magistrates of this city to attend the burning of some of the *Journals*, and which sets forth that they had been condemned by the Council to be burned by the hands of the common hangman. We much doubted the legality of these extraordinary proceedings of the Chief Justice and the rest of the Council. We saw the Chief Justice's name among those who issued that extraordinary warrant by which our client was apprehended. We had seen his want of moderation in demanding security in 800 pounds when Zenger was brought before him on his habeas corpus, though the act required bail to be taken only according to the quality of the prisoner and nature of the offense, and though at the same time this poor man had made oath before him that he was not worth 40 pounds, besides the tools of his trade and his apparel. We had heard the Chief Justice declare, in the fullest court we had then ever seen in that place, that if a jury found Zenger not guilty they would be perjured, or words to that effect; and this even before any information in form was lodged against him. As for Justice

Philipse, we had been told how vigorous and active he had been in the General Assembly to procure the concurrence of that House with the Council in the order for the burning of Zenger's papers, even before they were legally condemned, and in addressing the Governor to issue a proclamation with a promise of reward for the discovery of the writers of them, and in an order for prosecuting the poor printer.

We wish we had no occasion to repeat these things to show the motives of our conduct. Had we not been obliged thereto in order to vindicate ourselves, we had much rather that they had been buried in silence. But under these many forewarnings what could we do, what ought we to do, for our client? Surely everything that was lawful and likely to contribute to his safety.

Appendix III

James Alexander on Freedom of the Press

In 1737 the verdict of the Zenger trial was severely criticized in two anonymous letters to the *Barbados Gazette*, and these were reprinted by Andrew Bradford of Philadelphia. Alexander wrote a reply in the *Pennsylvania Gazette*. His essay is an important historical document, although strangely overlooked by the historians of American democracy. It presents him as the most important theorist of freedom of the press this country has ever produced. These are some of the key passages:

> Freedom of speech is a principal pillar in a free government. When this support is taken away, the Constitution is dissolved, and tyranny is erected on its ruins. Republics and limited monarchies derive their strength and vigor from a popular examination into the actions of the magistrates.

> These abuses of the freedom of speech are the excrescences of liberty. They ought to be suppressed; but to whom dare we commit the care of doing it? An evil magistrate, entrusted with a power to punish words, is armed with a weapon the most destructive and terrible. Under the pretense of pruning off the exuberant branches, he frequently destroys the tree.

> Augustus Caesar, under the specious pretext of preserving the characters of the Romans from defamation, introduced the law whereby libeling was involved in the penalties of treason against the state. This established his tyranny; and for one mischief it prevented, ten thousand evils, horrible and tremendous, sprang up in the place.

> Henry VIII, a prince mighty in politics, procured that act to be passed whereby the jurisdiction of the Star Chamber was confirmed and extended.... The subjects were terrified from uttering their griefs while they saw the thunder of the Star Chamber pointing at their heads. This caution, however, could not prevent several dangerous tumults and insurrections. For when the tongues of the people are restrained, they commonly discharge their resentments by a more dangerous organ, and break out into open acts of violence.

> But to resume the description of the reign of Charles II. The doctrine of servitude was chiefly managed by Sir Roger Lestrange. He had great advantages in the argument, being licenser for the press, and might have carried all before him without contradiction

if writings of the other side of the question had not been printed by stealth. The authors were prosecuted as seditious libelers.

In the two former papers the writer endeavored to prove by historical facts the fatal dangers that necessarily attend a restraint on freedom of speech and the liberty of the press: upon which the following reflection naturally occurs, viz., THAT WHOEVER ATTEMPTS TO SUPPRESS EITHER OF THOSE, OUR NATURAL RIGHTS, OUGHT TO BE REGARDED AS AN ENEMY TO LIBERTY AND THE CONSTITUTION.

In civil actions an advocate should never appear but when he is persuaded the merits of the cause lie on the side of his client. In criminal actions it often happens that the defendant in strict justice deserves punishment; yet a counsel may oppose it when a magistrate cannot come at the offender without making a breach in the barriers of liberty and opening a floodgate to arbitrary power. But when the defendant is innocent and unjustly prosecuted, his counsel may, nay ought to, take all advantages and use every stratagem that his skill, art, and learning can furnish him with. This last was the case of Zenger at New York, as appears by the printed trial and the verdict of the jury. It was a popular cause. The liberty of the press in that Province depended on it. On such occasions the dry rules of strict pleading are never observed. The counsel for the defendant sometimes argues from the known principles of law, then raises doubts and difficulties to confound his antagonist, now applies himself to the affections, and chiefly endeavors to raise the passions. Zenger's defense is to be considered in all those different lights.

Upon the whole: To suppress inquiries into the administration is good policy in an arbitrary government. But a free Constitution and freedom of speech have such a reciprocal dependence on each other that they cannot subsist without consisting together.

Notes to the Introduction

[1]Cadwallader Colden, *History of William Cosby's Administration as Governor of the Province of New York, and of Lieutenant-Governor George Clarke's Administration through 1737* (New York Historical Society Collections, 1935), p. 286.

[2]*Documents Relative to the Colonial History of the State of New York*, ed. E. B. O'Callaghan (Albany, 1853-87), V, 937.

[3]William Smith, *The History of the Late Province of New York, from Its Discovery to the Appointment of Governor Colden in 1762* (New York, 1829-30), II, 3.

[4]Livingston Rutherfurd, *John Peter Zenger, His Press, His Trial and a Bibliography of Zenger Imprints* (New York, 1904), p. 15.

[5]*N.Y. Col. Docs.*, V, 949.

[6]Colden, *op. cit.*, p. 298.

[7]*N.Y. Col. Docs.*, V, 955.

[8]Colden, *op. cit.*, pp. 298-299.

[9]*Ibid.*, p. 313.

[10]*New York Gazette*, November 5, 1733.

[11]*Ibid.*, January 7, 1734.

[12]*Ibid.*, March 18, 1734.

[13]*N.Y. Col. Docs.*, V, 940.

[14]*Documents Relating to the Colonial History of the State of New Jersey*, ed. William A. Whitehead (Newark, 1880-1928), V, 359.

[15]*Ibid.*, V, 360.

[16]*N.Y. Col. Docs.*, VI, 21.

[17]*Ibid.*, VI, 5.

[18]*New York Weekly Journal*, January 21, 1734.

[19]*Ibid.*, January 28, 1734.

[20]*New York Gazette*, February 4, 1734.

[21]*New York Weekly Journal*, November 26, 1733.

[22]*Ibid.*, December 31, 1733.

[23]*New York Gazette*, April 1, 1734.

[24]Colden, *op. cit.*, p. 323.

[25]*N.Y. Col. Docs.*, V, 978.

[26]*Ibid.*, V, 975.

[27]*Ibid.*, V, 976.

[28]*Ibid.*

[29]*Ibid.*

[30]*Ibid.*

[31]*Ibid.*, V, 984.

[32]*The Papers of Lewis Morris, Governor of the Province of New Jersey from 1738 to 1746*, ed. William A. Whitehead (New York, 1852), pp. 22-23.

[33]*Ibid.*, pp. 24-25.

[34]*N.Y. Col. Docs.*, VI, 21.

[35]*Ibid.*, VI, 34-35.

[36]Rutherfurd, *op. cit.*, pp. 127-128.

Notes to the Text

[1]William Hawkins was, during Zenger's own period, probably the outstanding author of legal textbooks. Delancey's quotations are from his *Treatise of the Pleas to the Crown* (London, 1724), I, 192-193.

[2]Henry Sacheverell, a Tory divine, attacked the Whig Ministry for not being Royalist or High Church enough. He was tried for seditious libel and found guilty (1710), but his case was instrumental in the decline of the Whigs and the rise of the Tories under Queen Anne. See G. N. Clark, *The Later Stuarts* (Oxford, 1940), pp. 216-217.

[3]Gilbert Burnet, Bishop of Salisbury, was the historian of his time as well as one of its most controversial ecclesiastico-politicians. His pastoral letter sounds innocuous enough now, but his enemies in Parliament impugned it as too Royalist and too favorable to the Dissenters (1693). See Macaulay's *History of England*, "Fireside" ed. (Boston and New York, 1910), IV, 464-466. Bishop Burnet was the father of New York's Governor William Burnet.

[4]Thomas Brewster, one of the many printers prosecuted during the reign of Charles II, was convicted (1663) of violating the licensing laws when he published *The Phoenix, or the Solemn League and Covenant*, which defended the regicides who executed Charles I. For Chief Justice Robert Hyde's excoriating summing up, see J. W. Willis-Bund, *A Selection of Cases from the State Trials* (Cambridge, 1882), II, 415.

[5]Sir John Holt, one of the great chief justices in the history of British law, handed down numerous important rulings on the subject of libel. See Fredrick Seaton Siebert, *Freedom of the Press in England, 1476-1776* (Urbana, Ill., 1952), *passim*.

[6]John Tutchin, publisher of the *Observator*, made broad charges of treason and corruption against the government, and was tried in a court presided over by Chief Justice Holt (1704). See Siebert, *op. cit.*, p. 275.

[7]William Fuller was one of the notorious impostors who abounded in England at the time of the Popish Plot. His grossly fictitious account of a sinister scheme to restore the Stuarts was exposed by the House of Commons (1692), and he was promptly arrested, prosecuted, and convicted. Macaulay has a good description of the Fuller incident, *op. cit.*, pp. 280-289.

[8]These ecclesiastics, led by William Sancroft, Archbishop of Canterbury, refused to promulgate from their pulpits the Declaration of Indulgence by which James II would have granted freedom of worship to his subjects. The Seven Bishops argued that he was attempting to exercise a dispensing power that the crown did not possess. They were prosecuted before Parliament, but acquitted (1688). See Clark, *op. cit.*, pp. 120-121.

[9]Francis Nicholson, a stormy petrel among colonial administrators, was Governor of Virginia at the time of this episode (1704). His intended victim was John Monroe, a clergyman of the Church of England. The information against Monroe is in the *Executive Journals of the Council of Virginia* (Richmond, 1927), II, 451-452.

[10]Laurence Echard, Tory divine and historian, wrote the bitterly anti-Williamite *History of the Revolution of 1688*. See Eugene Lawrence, *Lives of the British Historians* (New York, 1855), I, 312-315.

[11]Paul de Rapin de Thoyras, although a Frenchman, became the foremost authority on English history. His *Histoire d'Angleterre* appeared in 1723, and long remained the standard work on the subject, influencing a whole generation of British historians including Hume. See Lawrence, *op. cit.*, I, 226-229.

[12]Marcus Brutus, one of the assassins of Julius Caesar, is most familiar to the English-speaking world as Shakespeare's "noblest Roman of them all." Hamilton's anecdote is based on the laudatory picture of the man drawn in Plutarch's *Lives*.

[13]Lucius Junius Brutus was the Roman patriot who, according to legend, led the revolt that drove out Tarquin the Proud and put an end to the Kings of Rome. The story of his execution of his sons is told repeatedly by the Roman historians, the most familiar source being Livy's *History of Rome*, bk. I.

[14]John Hampden occupies a special niche in British history as the man who refused to pay the Ship Money levied by Charles I for the building of a fleet (1637). His defiance of the crown caught the imagination of later generations as a major step toward the development of parliamentary government in England. See George Macaulay Trevelyan, *England Under the Stuarts* (19th ed., London, 1947), p. 152.

Other Footnotes

[1]See Appendix I.

[2]Peter Zenger is the ostensible narrator throughout.
